What's Cooking at Moody's Diner

60 years of recipes and reminiscences

by Nancy Moody Genthner

edited by Kerry Leichtman

Dancing Bear Books

West Rockport, ME

Library of Congress Cataloging in Publication Data
Genthner, Nancy Moody, 1935-
        What's Cooking at Moody's Diner

        Includes index.
        1. Cookery, American.   2. Moody's Diner—History.
3. Cookery—Maine—Waldoboro.   4. Moody family.
I. Leichtman, Kerry. II. Title
TX715.G347 1989   641.5973   89-50228
ISBN 0-88448-075-5

Dancing Bear Books
P.O. Box 4
West Rockport, Maine 04865
Printed in the United States of America
10 9 8

Dancing Bear Books are distributed by Tilbury House, Publishers
The Boston Building, 132 Water Street, Gardiner, Maine 04345.

Book designed in cooperation with Outstandingly Graphic, Rockland, ME.
Page-corner animations by Rod McCormick, Rockland, ME.
Cover art by Paul Amtmann, Camden, ME.
PostScript image setting by High Resolution, Camden, ME, 236-3777.

1902 - 1977

This cookbook is lovingly dedicated to our mother, Bertha Moody, and contains many of her favorite recipes. Mom was teaching in a one-room schoolhouse in North Nobleboro, Maine when she met and married Dad. That was in 1922. She was the steady force behind the scenes in Dad's many business ventures, and in each one of our lives.

In the diner's early days, Mom did all the baking at home either late in the evening or early morning. Summers she managed the cabins, renting units, taking reservations, supervising the cabin girls and cooking a main meal each day for the family and summer help, which meant 12-14 people around the table. In the fall she ran the house and business herself as Dad was away for three months cutting Christmas trees. In the midst of all this, Mom raised nine children, kept a pantry stocked with homemade donuts, cookies and other goodies for us to enjoy. It has always amazed me, in thinking about her life, that she did all of this without the benefit of automatic washers and dryers, microwaves, etc., and yet each of us felt loved, special and cared for.

We all have memories of her at the kitchen table after supper helping with homework, packing lunches for school in the morning, frying dozens of donuts each week, making birthday cakes, of always being there for us. She was a special lady who will always be remembered with much love and gratitude from each of her children.

**Proverbs 31:28 Her children shall
rise up and bless her.**

Table of Contents

Introduction

 national icon, a vintage 1930's diner, that's how they describe Moody's Diner. Two stories come to mind that are so similar I can tell them together. In one a television station from away called to say they wanted to do a feature on Moody's Diner as part of a series featuring restaurants across America. Moody's was to be their choice representing Maine. The other story involves a major women's/home magazine. The television station and the magazine each wanted to capture the simple country folk Americana that is Moody's Diner.

The television people asked Nancy Moody Genthner for a New England food that could be prepared on the air. She sent them some recipes. They responded by telling her they were too simple, they needed to use 15 minutes of air time. "But none of our foods take that long to prepare," she told them.

The magazine's food editor called one day and said they wanted to fly a production crew up to Maine the following Monday to photograph the making of New England Boiled Dinner at Moody's Diner. Nancy told them they were welcome to come and take the pictures, but Moody's cooked and served boiled dinner on Thursdays, so come then. "Don't worry," she was told, "and no slight intended to your chef, but we're bringing our own meat and recipe, we just need to use your kitchen Monday morning at 11:00." The editor was probably surprised when Alvah Moody got on the phone and said if they wanted to photograph the preparation of a Moody's Diner New England Boiled Dinner they could show up on Thursday — without the groceries.

Those of you who have been to Moody's Diner know that Moody's is not a quaint-on-purpose tourist attraction, nor is it a food editor's prop. It is a diner on U.S. 1 in Waldoboro, Maine, plain and simple. It has survived, prospered and grown these 60 some odd years because of good food, reasonable prices and quick, pleasant service. There are people who eat at Moody's every day, and those who come in every time they travel to Maine. Both are made welcome. Locals aren't expected to go elsewhere during tourist season and tourists aren't gouged for their vacation cash.

The country has changed these past 60 years. There have been 11 U.S. Presidents, we've been involved in three major wars, swooned to Frank Sinatra and danced with the Beatles, sent men to the moon, and have known countless fads and styles, from crewcuts and the hoola hoop to video games and pet rocks. Yet Moody's has endured.

The American dream is success achieved through hard work and honesty. Moody's Diner encompasses that ideal.

Alvah Moody, who you'll meet later in this book, says success came because, "It was the only place open 24 hours between Bangor and Portland before they built the interstate, back when Route 1 was the highway." But Alvah was only telling half the story. I once asked 89-year old P.B. Moody, who you see in the photo below, if he was surprised by how successful Moody's Diner had become. His response was quick, "Of course not, it's run by Moodys."

Marian Savage, who took some of the photographs you'll see in the pages ahead, said P.B. used to scrub the kitchen floor by hand to make sure it got done right. Alvah figured that if you roast a turkey upside down its juices would flow toward the breast and make that dry portion of meat juicier. That's what you're served at Moody's, along with fresh mashed potatoes, gravy made from a recipe rather than a jar and a dessert favorite like Lemon Meringue or Walnut pie. That's why the trucks still stop at Moody's Diner, despite I-95, and why tourists keep Moody's on their Maine itineraries, and why some people eat at Moody's Diner every day.

The Moody's are a large family. Most of them have worked at the diner, many of them still do. They run the diner like a restaurant, not a museum, serving good food; fast, hot and inexpensively. In *What's Cooking at Moody's Diner*, they are sharing 60 years of memories, photos and... oh yes, recipes. They're authentic all right, take a look at the quantity of ingredients called for.

Most of the Moody's Diner recipes originated with Bertha Moody. Nancy has also included recipes gathered from the entire Moody family and from a few longtime diner employees. Some of the recipes have titles like Aunt Bertha's Casserole, or Mom's Cookies, or Grandma's Muffins — remembering other Bertha Moody favorites.

Whether you're from down the road or across the country, we'll see you next time you stop at Moody's.

—Kerry Leichtman

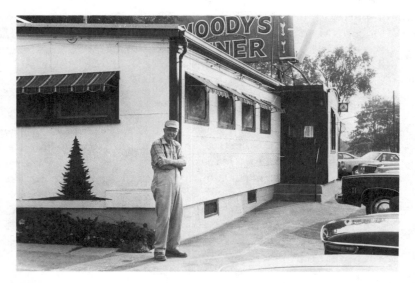

Marian Savage

Moody's Diner Recipes

Moody's Diner 1935

Rod McCormick

The ingredients listed with most of the Moody's Diner recipes are proportioned for, as the expression goes, feeding an army. To translate them down to family-size portions consider the following equivalents: there are 16 cups to the gallon, 16 tbsp. to the cup and 3 tsp. to the tbsp.

Moody's Fish Chowder

25 lbs. Norwegian haddock fillets	12 cans (12 oz.) evaporated milk
10 quarts diced potatoes	1 1/2 pints all-purpose cream
8 cups chopped onion	1/2 lb. oleo
salt and pepper	

Place fish in large kettle; cover with water and cook until fish flakes apart. Remove fish. Add potatoes and onions to stock (if necessary, add more water to cover potatoes), and cook until potatoes are tender. Add milk, cream, oleo, salt and pepper. Add cooked, flaked fish. Let stand 1 hour over low heat to blend flavor.

New England Boiled Dinner

1, 10 lb. corned bottom round	30 whole peeled carrots
30 peeled potatoes	30 slices EACH turnip and cabbage

Place corned round in pressure cooker and cook 35 minutes at 15 lbs. Remove meat to steam table. Put vegetables in pressure cooker and cook 15 minutes at 15 lbs. Place vegetables in steam table. Serve 3 slices corned beef with potato, carrot, cabbage and turnip. Serve with vinegar and mustard, and a side of buttered beets.

Moody's Meatloaf

10 lbs. ground beef　10 eggs
3 cups chopped onion　1 1/2 quarts milk
1/2 lb. crushed saltines　salt and pepper
4 cans (10 oz.) tomato soup

Combine ground beef, onions and saltines. Stir in eggs, milk and seasoning. Divide meat into 4 large loaf pans. Bake 30 minutes at 350 degrees. Remove from oven and pour tomato soup over meatloaf. Return to oven and bake 1 hour longer.

Vegetable Beef Stew

5 lbs. stew beef　4 cups chopped cabbage
8 cups diced carrots　2 pkgs. Beef Onion Soup mix
8 cups diced turnip　1 can (8 oz.) vegetable juice
4 quarts diced potatoes　1 can (15 oz.) stewed tomatoes
4 cups chopped onion　1 can (15 oz.) red kidney beans
4 cups chopped celery　1 can (15 oz.) lima beans
4 cups frozen peas　salt and pepper

Brown stew beef in pressure cooker, then cover with water and cook 20 minutes at 15 lbs. Let set in refrigerator until fat rises to the top. Skim fat and remove meat from stock. Add carrots and turnip to stock and cook until tender. If necessary, add more water to stock, to cover vegetables. Add remaining ingredients and cook until potatoes are tender. Combine 2 cups flour and water to make a wash, and add to broth; simmer until thickened. Season with salt and pepper.

Pea Soup

2 gallons water　4 cups chopped onions
7 pkgs. (1 lb.) dried peas　4 cups ham, cut in bite-sized pieces
salt and pepper

Combine all ingredients in large kettle and simmer 1 1/2 hours over low heat. Stir occasionally.

Johnny Cake

8 cups flour　1 tsp. salt
5 tbsp. baking powder　1 cup melted shortening
3 cups cornmeal　5 eggs
5 cups milk

Beat together eggs and milk, and stir in dry ingredients. Mix well and add melted shortening. Pour batter into greased 12 x 18 pan and bake 1 hour at 350 degrees.

Moody's Mincemeat

3 cups cooked ground meat	2 1/2 cups hot, instant coffee
9 cups ground apples	1/2 cup vinegar
1 lb. ground seeded raisins	1 tsp. salt
1 lb. whole seedless raisins	2 tsp. cloves
3/4 lb. oleo	2 tsp. cinnamon
6 cups sugar	2 tsp. nutmeg
1 tsp. allspice	

Combine all ingredients in large kettle and cook over a moderate heat. Stir often, as mincemeat will easily burn. Cook approximately one hour, or until mixture darkens. Seal in jars while hot.

Moody's Apple Cobbler

6 cups flour	4 eggs
1 tsp. salt	3 cups milk
1 cup sugar	1 cup melted shortening
4 tbsp. baking powder	10-12 cups sliced apples

Topping:

1 cup sugar	1 tbsp. cinnamon
4 tbsp. oleo	

Sauce:

1 lb. oleo	4 cups sugar
6 cups water	3/4 cup cornstarch
2 tsp. vanilla or lemon flavoring	

Sift together flour, salt, sugar and baking powder. Beat eggs, add milk and beat again. Pour eggs and milk into dry ingredients, add melted shortening and stir well. Pour batter into greased 12 x 18 pan and cover with sliced apples.

Combine topping ingredients; sprinkle over batter and dot with oleo. Bake 30-40 minutes at 350 degrees. Serve warm, topped with sauce.

Sauce — In large saucepan, melt oleo in water. Combine cornstarch and sugar in small bowl. Add approximately 2 tbsp. cool water and blend into a smooth paste. Stir in hot water, return to saucepan and bring to a boil. Cook a few minutes, until thickened. Remove from heat and add flavoring. Serve over hot apple cobbler.

When it first started out it was just a little stand with an open serving window. Then he put a little porch over the front of it. When he moved it down to the new Route 1 he went over the whole thing and wound up with a door at each end. That original counter is still in the center up to the cash register.

Then he added on the back of it, and put in the ladies and men's rooms. Then he built on a piece at the back for a woodshed. The next year he continued the end where the horseshoe counter is now and made a dining room, and he added the little piece on the front for the door. Next he put in the horseshoe counter, and in '48 he put in the dining room at the other end. That was the last time the appearance of the place changed on the outside. The outside was changed probably 7 times since the original. There were a lot of things done on the inside. The back wall was moved back a couple of times, 3 or 4 feet at a time.

In '49 we moved the back wall of the kitchen out. It was the year I built my house. I took my crew over on a Saturday night and we cut the wall right out, put it on some pipes and rolled it right out. we studded up the roof, had the fans right on the wall, we had an electrician there extending the wires, and started right in cooking the next morning. Bill Jones said I'd get lost with all that new space in there. We moved it back 5 feet and it seemed like we had all kinds of room. -- Alvah Moody

Over the years there have been many Moody's Diner postcards. P.B. Moody used to write the copy, like the following taken from the back of the above card:

The management of Moody's Cabins extends a hearty welcome to all to spend a night, or an entire vacation, at the famous cabins.'

We are situated on a high hill overlooking the surrounding country, with a delightful view at 50 to 100 miles of rugged country. We offer comfortable, roomy cabins for two, three and four people. All have running water, screened porches and Simmon's beds. Most of the cabins have equipment for wood fires when desired. Some have flush toilets and showers, others have fully equipped kitchenette for light housekeeping. Dining room on grounds. We think it is a jolly good place for a vacation. Come and see.

Patrick Downs

Apple Crisp

2 cups oatmeal 1 tbsp. cinnamon
2 cups sugar 3/4 lb. oleo
2 1/4 cups flour 14-16 cups sliced apples

Line a greased 12 x 18 pan with 3/4-inch layer of apples. Combine oatmeal, sugar, flour and cinnamon in large bowl. Cut in oleo until mixture resembles coarse crumbs and sprinkle over apples. Cook 35-30 minutes at 350 degrees. Serve hot, topped with whipped cream.

Bread Pudding

14 eggs 1 tbsp. cinnamon
6 quarts milk 1/2 tsp. salt
1 cup sugar 3 tsp. vanilla
1 tbsp. nutmeg 1/2 lb. raisins
40 slices of bread, cut into small pieces

Beat eggs; add milk and sugar, and stir well. Stir in spices and vanilla. Arrange bread in large, deep casserole dish. Pour egg and milk batter over bread and stir. Stir in raisins. Bake 2 1/2 hours at 350 degrees, stirring occasionally.

Grapenut Custard Pudding

12 eggs 1 tsp. vanilla
3 cups sugar 1 tsp. salt
2 1/4 cups grapenuts 3 quarts milk

Beat eggs; add sugar, salt, vanilla and grapenuts and mix well. Stir in milk. Pour into 12 x 18 pan and bake 1 hour at 350 degrees.

Grapenut Pudding

1 gallon milk 10 tbsp. flour
1 box (16 oz.) grapenuts 8 eggs, separated
2 cups sugar 1/4 cup sugar

In top of double boiler, combine and heat milk and grapenuts. In large bowl, mix together 2 cups sugar, egg yolks and flour. Add a little milk to make a smooth paste, then add to warm milk in double boiler. Cook until thickened. In separate bowl, beat egg whites. When nearly stiff, add remaining sugar and beat until egg whites are stiff. Fold egg whites into cooked pudding. Serve with whipped cream.

Indian Pudding

1 gallon milk	2 cups molasses
1/4 lb. oleo	2 cups cornmeal
6 eggs	1 tbsp. cinnamon
1 3/4 cups sugar	1 tbsp. vanilla
1/2 lb. raisins	

Reserve 1 cup of milk and heat remainder with oleo. In large bowl, beat eggs and reserved milk. Mix in sugar, molasses, cornmeal, cinnamon and vanilla. Combine with warmed milk and stir in raisins. Bake pudding in large kettle 2 hours at 350 degrees. Stir often during first 30 minutes of baking to prevent cornmeal sticking.

Tapioca Pudding

4 quarts milk	2 cups sugar
1/4 lb. oleo	1 tsp. salt
10 eggs, separated	2 cups tapioca
1 tsp. vanilla	

Heat milk and oleo in double boiler. In large bowl, beat egg yolks with 1 1/2 cups sugar, salt and tapioca, then add to heated milk. Cook 5 minutes, stirring well. Remove from heat and add vanilla. Beat egg whites with remaining sugar until stiff and fold into hot pudding.

Steamed Pudding with Sweet Sauce

We always serve this pudding with Thanksgiving Dinner at Moody's.

1 pint breadcrumbs	1 beaten egg
1/4 cup molasses	1 tsp. baking soda
1 cup milk	2 tbsp. flour
1 cup chopped raisins	

Sweet Sauce:

1 egg	1/3 cup melted oleo
1 cup sugar	1 tsp. vanilla

Combine all pudding ingredients, mix well and pour into greased 1 lb. coffee can. Steam 2 hours. Remove pudding from pan, slice and top with Sweet Sauce. To make sauce, combine egg, sugar, oleo and vanilla, and beat 2-3 minutes. Pour over hot slices of pudding.

Bran Muffins

6 cups all-bran	5 cups flour
5 cups milk	2 tsp. salt
4 eggs	2 cups sugar
1 1/3 cups melted shortening	4 tbsp. baking powder

Combine bran and milk; stir and let set a few minutes. Add shortening and eggs, and stir well. Sift together dry ingredients and add to batter. Mix well. Pour batter into greased muffin cups, 3/4-full, and bake 20 minutes at 400 degrees.

Moody's Blueberry Muffins

6 cups flour	3 eggs
4 tbsp. baking powder	1 cup melted shortening
1 1/2 tsp. salt	3 cups milk
1 cup sugar	2 cups blueberries

Mix together flour, baking powder, sugar and salt. Set aside. Beat eggs; add milk and combine with dry ingredients. Add melted shortening and mix well. Dust blueberries with flour and fold into batter. Fill greased muffins tins 3/4-full. Bake 20 minutes at 400 degrees.

Date Muffins

6 cups flour	3 cups milk
4 tbsp. baking powder	1 cup melted shortening
1 1/2 tsp. salt	3 eggs
1 cup sugar	1 1/4 cup date filling

Sift together dry ingredients. In large bowl, beat eggs, add milk and combine with dry ingredients. Mix thoroughly and stir in melted shortening. Fold in date filling and pour batter into greased muffin cups, 3/4-full. Bake 20 minutes at 400 degrees.

Pineapple Muffins

6 cups flour	2 cups milk
4 tbsp. baking powder	1 cup melted shortening
1 1/2 tsp. salt	1 cup pineapple juice
1 cup sugar	3 eggs
2 cans (20 oz.) crushed pineapple	

Sift together dry ingredients and set aside. Beat eggs in separate bowl. Add milk and pineapple juice and combine with dry ingredients. Mix thoroughly. Stir in melted shortening and fold in crushed pineapple. Pour batter into greased muffin tins, 3/4-full and bake 20 minutes at 400 degrees.

Plain Doughnuts

2 cups sugar	1 tsp. vanilla
3 tbsp. melted oleo	5-7 cups flour
4 eggs	4 tsp. baking powder
2 cups milk	1 1/2 tsp. nutmeg
1 1/4 tsp. salt	

Beat eggs with sugar, oleo and vanilla. Mix in milk, 3 cups flour and remaining dry ingredients. Add remaining flour until dough is soft enough to handle. Turn dough onto floured surface and roll. Cut with doughnut cutter and fry in hot fat.

Chocolate Doughnuts

1 1/4 cups sugar	1 tsp. salt
3 tbsp. melted oleo	1 tsp. baking soda
2 eggs	1/8 tsp. ginger
1 cup buttermilk OR sour milk	2 heaping tbsp. cocoa
1 tsp. baking powder	1 1/2 tsp. vanilla
4 cups flour	

Beat together eggs, sugar, oleo and vanilla. Add milk and stir. Sift dry ingredients and add to batter. Roll dough on floured surface and cut with doughnut cutter. Cook in hot fat.

Nancy Moody Genthner: *Mom used to make this recipe, plus a batch of plain or molasses doughnuts, each week when we were growing up. There was always a big can of assorted doughnuts on the shelf in the cellarway. She cooked them in a big blue agate kettle. I can still remember the smell of hot doughnuts in the kitchen when we came home from school.*

Alvah Moody: *She used to go down to the diner and fry doughnuts and serve them to the people right there. She'd fry plain, chocolate and molasses. She used to take doughnuts right out of the kettle and the people would sit there and eat them.*

Nellie Moody Jones: *Do you remember when the donuts used to sit in the cellar-way? Now who was it that knocked the can downstairs with the donuts in it?*

Alvah: *One of us kids didn't put the kettle back all the way on the shelf.*

Nellie: *Uncle George knocked it over I think. He went into the cellar with a stove poker to get them.*

Alvah: *He came up the stairs with all the donuts skewered on the poker and said, "Here are your donuts Bertha." There were cobwebs hanging from them. I can remember that as plain as anything.*

Brownies

3 3/4 sticks oleo	2 tsp. vanilla
6 squares unsweetened chocolate	1 1/2 tsp. salt
3 cups sugar	1 1/2 tsp. baking powder
6 eggs	1 cup chopped nuts
2 1/2 cups flour	

Melt together chocolate and oleo; set aside to cool. In large bowl, cream sugar and eggs, then add cooled chocolate. Beat. Mix in vanilla, salt, baking powder, flour and chopped nuts. Pour into ungreased 12 x 8 baking pan and bake 20 minutes at 375 degrees.

Peanut Butter Cupcakes

3/4 cup shortening	2 cups milk
1 cup peanut butter	2 tsp. vanilla
2 cups sugar	4 cups flour
5 eggs	2 tsp. salt
5 tsp. baking powder	

Combine and cream shortening, peanut butter, sugar and eggs until smooth. Add milk, vanilla, flour, salt and baking powder, and mix well. Line muffin tins with cupcake papers and pour batter into papers, 3/4-full. Bake 20 minutes at 375 degrees.

Chocolate Cupcakes

3/4 cup shortening	1 3/4 cups milk
3/4 cup sugar	3 1/2 cups flour
6 eggs	5 tsp. baking powder
2 tsp. vanilla	1 cup cocoa
2 tsp. salt	

Combine and cream shortening, sugar, eggs and vanilla until smooth. Add milk, flour, baking powder, cocoa and salt. Mix thoroughly. Pour batter into lined muffin tins, 3/4-full. Bake 20 minutes at 375 degrees.

Banana Cupcakes

1 1/2 cups oleo	2 cups mashed bananas
3 cups sugar	1/2 cup milk
4 eggs	4 cups flour
2 tsp. vanilla	2 tsp. baking soda
1 tsp. salt	

Combine and cream oleo, sugar, eggs and vanilla. Add milk, bananas, flour, baking soda and salt. Mix well. Pour batter into lined muffin tins, 3/4-full. Bake 15-20 minutes at 400 degrees.

Moody's Ice Cream

27 egg yolks	4 tsp. salt
10 cups sugar	7 quarts milk
3 tbsp. gelatin	2 quarts cream
4 cans (12 oz.) evaporated milk	

Beat eggs yolks; add sugar, gelatin and salt, and beat again. Heat milk in double boiler. When hot, stir in egg mixture and cook until batter coats spoon. Add cream, evaporated milk and flavoring. Freeze. *We made many flavors. Be creative.*

Alvah: *We made our own mix until '43 or '44 but then stopped because of sugar rationing.* Nancy: *All the ice cream freezers were in a room at the back of the garage. There was a little hole in the floor. Dad bottled his own milk then so there were bottle caps in there. As kids we used to dip into the ice cream with the bottle caps and then throw the bottle caps through the hole. When they tore that building down there was a huge pile of bottle caps. Dad always wondered where they came from.*

Basic Cream Pie

3 cups milk	2 tbsp. flour
1/4 cup oleo	3 tbsp. cornstarch
2 eggs	dash of salt
1 cup sugar	1 tsp. vanilla

Heat milk and oleo in double boiler. In medium bowl, beat together eggs and sugar. Add flour, cornstarch, salt and vanilla and mix well. Pour egg mixture into double boiler with hot milk and stir until thickened. Cool and pour into baked 9-inch pie shell.
Banana Cream: Line bottom of baked pie shell with sliced bananas. Cover with cream filling and top with whipped cream.
Coconut Cream: Add 1 cup shredded coconut to cream filling. Pour into baked pie shell and top with whipped cream.
Peanut Butter Pie: Add 1 cup peanut butter to filling and blend well. Pour into pie shell and top with whipped cream.
Each pie recipe makes 2 pies.

Moody's Chocolate Cream Pie

3 cups milk	3 tbsp. cornstarch
1/4 cup oleo	3 eggs
1 cup sugar	3 tbsp. cocoa OR 2 tbsp. cocoa
2 tbsp. flour	and one square (2 oz.) chocolate
	1 tsp. vanilla

Heat milk and oleo in double boiler. (If using chocolate squares, melt them in the milk.) Mix sugar, flour, cornstarch, cocoa and eggs, and pour into heated milk. Stir well until thickened. Add vanilla and stir. Pour into cooked pie shells and chill until firm. Top with whipped cream. See Pies chapter for pie crust recipes.

Moody's Blueberry Pie

4 cups fresh blueberries	cinnamon or nutmeg to taste
1 tbsp. flour	dash of salt
1 cup sugar	2 tbsp. butter
	2 tbsp. milk

Pour blueberries into unbaked 9-inch pie shells. Mix dry ingredients and pour over berries. Dot with butter. Cover with top crust that has been dusted with flour and brushed with milk. Bake 30-35 minutes at 350 degrees.

Greetings from Cairo, Egypt!
We're enclosing a couple of photos taken in front of the Sphinx and Pyramid of Chefron in Giza, Egypt.   We've been living here since last July. Soon after arriving, I was at a company function wearing my Moody's Diner T-shirt. A guy walked up to me and said, "Excuse me, but I have to introduce myself to anyone wearing a Moody's T-shirt in Egypt."
---From a letter from Mark & Neila Brownstein

Moody's Custard Pie

8 eggs	1 level tbsp. flour
1 cup sugar	1 tsp. salt
1 tsp. nutmeg	5 cups milk

In large bowl, beat eggs with flour, salt, sugar and nutmeg. Stir in milk and pour batter through strainer into deep, unbaked, 9-inch pie shells. Bake 15 minutes at 400 degrees, then reduce heat to 325 and bake 25-30 minutes or until pie is set.
This recipe makes one pie.

"Your Walnut Cream Pie is the best I've ever eaten.
I've been to many parts of the world, your's is the best.
Now comes the hard part, do you think I might please *have the recipe."*
--Letter from Mrs. Betsy Baker of Plymouth, MA January 1989

Moody's Walnut Pie

3/4 cup melted oleo	2 cups chopped walnuts
9 eggs	1 1/2 cups sugar
3/4 tsp. salt	3 heaping tbsp. flour
2 cups milk	2 1/2 cups dark corn syrup
1 1/2 tsp. vanilla	

In large bowl, beat together melted oleo, sugar, eggs, flour, salt, vanilla and corn syrup. Beat well and stir in milk. Spread nuts in each uncooked, 9-inch pie shell. Pour batter over nuts. Bake 30-40 minutes at 350 degrees. Makes two 9-inch pies.

Gourmet

October 30, 1987

Dear Chef de Cuisine:

We have received an enthusiastic letter from one of our readers about the fine food you serve in your restaurant. Our correspondent particularly admired the Walnut Cream Pie.

We wonder if you would be so gracious as to share the recipe with us. If you would like to do so, and if at some time your recipe is chosen for publication in GOURMET MAGAZINE, we will credit your restaurant and send you a complimentary copy of the issue in which the recipe appears. The decision whether or not to publish a recipe is based upon editorial needs each month.

Thank you for your time and consideration.

Sincerely yours,

Ladd Boris
Editorial Assistant

A CONDÉ NAST PUBLICATION
560 LEXINGTON AVENUE•NEW YORK, NY 10022•(212) 371-1330

Moody's Diner Assists Santa For Third Year

Although Santa Claus gets busy only once a year the staff at Moody's Diner make their Christmas giving a year around affair. For the past three years the entire staff has seen that every local boy received a remembrance from the Diner where they used to drop in so frequently.

The first year the staff chipped in and made delicious home-made fruitcakes and 'the Christmas package contained cigarettes and fruitcake, sent to servicemen.

Last year the ingredients for fruitcakes wre lacking so that home-made candy and cigarettes went out to all corners of the globe.

This year it 'will again be fruitcakes and cigarettes and every local boy has been remembered, although doubtful addresses may receive only a card -- at least the staff at Moody's has remembered them all. In talking 'with P. B. Moody who professed to know "little about it" and "have little to do with it", "They handle 'it all themselves and any boy local or otherwise who has an address on file will be remembered".

The waitresses, chefs, the pastry cook, and the dishwashers all contribute a portion of their paychecks each week throughout the year so that they may have a fund sufficient to remember all the boys in blue and khaki. The addresses are sought 'with painstaking care and each package carefully wrapped and addressed.

The entire project is voluntary on the part 'of the staff. Mrs. Nellie Benner acts as a co-ordinator for the project. Hats off to these busy people who still have time and inclination to make this friendly gesture!

Nellie: *When the servicemen came down from Limestone that day, we closed the diner there were so many of them. It was the middle of the afternoon in winter time. A great big convoy of them. Oh it was cold — there was snow and the wind was blowing. They were in open command cars. The back was closed, but only with canvas, and where the men drove it was completely open. It was really cold. They all had facemasks on.*

Dad closed the diner and Clara came up and we made more donuts and we laid everything out and they came in one door and went out the other, a line of them picking up food as they walked through.

Alvah: *During the '40's they had patrols all the time, day and night, all along the coast.*

Before I went into the Navy I used to go up to the lookout station at night. We were supposed to watch for airplanes. I was 15 or 16 years old at the time. Windows were all covered with black gauze so the lights wouldn't shine outside. The civil defense groups all wore black clothes in the streets. They had flashlights that were almost all covered so they only made a small spot of light on the ground.

The Army used to check to make sure civil defense people were at their posts. They went all over the coast.

Bill Jones: *Everyone took it seriously. They thought the Germans would land submarines here on the coast.*

Alvah: *It was quite exciting.*

From the scrapbook of Nellie Moody Jones. Exact date of publication unknown.

Fruitcake

This was the cake Nellie Benner baked and sent to the many servicemen from Waldoboro serving in World War II.

4 eggs	1 tsp. cinnamon
2 cups sugar	1 tsp. cloves
1 cup oleo	1 cup milk
3 3/4 cups flour	1 lb. chopped raisins
1 tsp. baking powder	1 lb. chopped dates
1 tsp. nutmeg	1 lb. chopped walnuts
candied fruit, optional	

Beat together eggs, sugar and oleo. Stir in milk. Sift dry ingredients and add to batter. Fold in chopped fruit and nuts, and stir in candied fruit. Pour batter into two greased and floured loaf pans. Bake 50-60 minutes at 350 degrees.

And today's special will be fish and chips. P.B. Moody (right) and his brother-in-law Irving Eaton show off a day's catch.

Marian Savage

In April of 1976 Mom compiled this history of the family business:

* * * * *

In 1927 we built three small cabins. Each had one room and a screened porch with dry toilets up back. There was no running water then; we bought spring water from Mack's Bottle Works in town and took a glass jug of cold water to guests when they came in. The cabins rented for $1.00 per person — that was before the days of sales tax. Since we had no eating place we sent people downtown to Brown's Restaurant under the old Star Theater.

Business was good. So the next year we built two two-room cabins and two more one-room cabins. The one-room cabins were fitted out with twin beds. We rented those rooms for $3.00 ($1.50 per person).

The next year, 1929, we drilled a well and built a building for showers and toilets. By 1939 we had our present number of cabins, and all had bathrooms.

During those first years the cabins had no heat, but soon all were equipped with wood stoves. Our sons went around with a wheelbarrow and filled the boxes. Later we installed gas heaters in some of the cabins. Now all have thermostat-controlled electric heat.

In the summer of 1930 we bought a small house by the entrance to the cabins and opened a small restaurant, serving only breakfast and dinner. Next, we installed gasoline pumps in front of the restaurant. The road in front of the cabins and restaurant was Route 1, now it's 1A. In either 1931 or '32 we put a very small lunch wagon next to the restaurant and sold hot dogs and hamburgers through the day.

In August 1934 the present Route 1 was opened. We had to buy land there that adjoined ours and then built a road to connect our business with Route 1. That was where the present Moody's Diner was born.

We moved the little lunch wagon down to the new Route 1, put a screened porch on the front and were ready for business when the new road opened. We only served lunch during the first year, and I cooked all the pastry myself at home.

As the business grew we added sections to the little lunch wagon until reaching its present size with a full basement, a pastry kitchen, seating capacity for 70, and central air conditioning. We kept the little restaurant on the hill beside the cabins open for just two summers after the small diner was opened.

* * * * *

Most people know Dad as P.B. He was born in 1900 in North Nobleboro, the youngest of seven children. He attended high school at Lincoln Academy, traveling by horse and buggy to the train station and from there to the academy in Damariscotta. His parents took in summer boarders for vacations at their home on Damariscotta Lake, so he fell in quite naturally to the tourist business.

Dad moved to Waldoboro when he and Mom married in 1922. He seemed to have boundless energy and thrived on hard work. He'd catnap in his Morris chair for 15 minutes and then jump up refreshed to tackle another job. In the early years he did many things to earn a living; peddling fish door to door, smelting, raising vegetables for a roadside stand, to mention a few.

When he started the diner he kept a large vegetable garden, raised beef steers and pigs, hayed and kept dairy animals for both the family and the business. In the fall he'd leave home for three months to continue his father's Christmas tree business. He'd come home every Saturday night and leave again on Sunday. Mom had the responsibility to care for the children and the diner. She also handled the phone orders for Christmas trees.

Each year Dad would ship 5-6 carloads of Christmas trees (about 5,000 trees) by rail to the old Charlestown freight yard in Boston. Mom would accompany him and my uncle to Boston for two weeks in early December to sell the trees. They stayed at a rooming house on Mass. Avenue with Dad going off to the freight yard each morning and Mom going by subway into Boston to do her Christmas shopping. I have often thought what a vacation that must have been for her, to be relieved of caring for all of us and to think only of herself and Dad, and best of all to eat all of her meals out!

It was with great excitement that we would watch for them to arrive home from Boston. They would drive in, the car loaded with the results of Mom's shopping. Dad would smell of fir. We'd watch with anticipation as the car was unpacked. The smell of fir today ushers in those memories of the exciting days before Christmas at our house.

In December 1954, while I was attending college in Providence, Rhode Island, I went by train to Boston and spent a weekend with my parents during their annual two weeks there. It was a great experience to see my parents in these unusual surroundings. I have never forgotten it.

—— Appetizers ——

Chili Con Queso

1 cup finely chopped onion	2 tbsp. chili powder
1 tsp. shortening	1/2 tsp. oregano
1 lg. ripe tomato, finely chopped	1/2 tsp. salt
2 medium green chilis, finely chopped	3/4 lb. grated Cheddar cheese

Saute onion in melted shortening; add tomatoes, green chilis, spices and salt. Cook 10 minutes over low heat. Add cheese and heat until melted. If necessary, add a little milk for desired consistency. Pour dip into fondue pan or chafing dish to keep it warm, and serve with tortilla chips.
—Charlene Ward

Cheese Ball

2 pkgs. (8 oz.) cream cheese	1 jar (5 oz.) blue cheese spread
1 jar (4 oz.) port wine cheese spread	1 tsp. Worcestershire sauce
1/4 cup chopped nuts	

Bring all ingredients to room temperature and combine. Mix well. Shape cheese into a ball and then roll in nuts. Chill before serving with crackers.
—Gail Kennedy

Cheese Ball II

1 pkg. (8 oz.) cream cheese	1 jar (4 oz.) pineapple cheese spread
1 jar (4 oz.) Cheddar cheese spread	1/4 cup chopped onion
1 jar (4 oz.) pimento cheese	1/4 cup chopped walnuts

Bring all ingredients to room temperature and combine. Mix well and shape cheese into a ball. Roll in nuts and chill before serving.
—Charlene Ward

Lorraine's Beef Dip

1 lb. ground beef 1/4 cup catsup
1/2 cup chopped onions 3/4 tsp. crushed oregano
1 clove minced garlic 1 tsp. sugar
1 can (8 oz.) tomato sauce 1 pkg. (8 oz.) cream cheese
1/3 cup grated Cheddar cheese

Cook together ground beef, onions and garlic. Drain meat and stir in remaining ingredients, except cheeses. Simmer 10 minutes and remove from heat. Add cheeses and stir. Serve warm with nacho chips.
—Rebecca Little

Taco Dip

1 pkg. (8 oz.) softened cream cheese 1 pkg. taco seasoning mix
1 cup grated Cheddar cheese 1 cup shredded lettuce
1 cup sour cream 1 diced tomato

Combine cream cheese, sour cream and taco seasoning. Beat well and spread in 9 x 13 pan. Top with lettuce, tomato and grated cheese. Serve with taco chips.
—Anne Braley

Nellie and Nancy
outside the diner.

Chutney Spread

2 pkgs. (8 oz.) cream cheese	1 tsp. curry powder
1/2 cup chopped, toasted almonds	1/2 tsp. dry mustard
1/2 cup prepared chutney	

Combine all ingredients and blend until smooth. Pour into small bowl and chill until firm. Serve with crackers.
—Dorothy Bruns Moody

Bread and Butter Pickles

25 med. cucumbers	1/2 cup water
10 med. onions, sliced	2 cups sugar
1/2 cup salt	2 tsp. mustard seed
3 cups vinegar	2 tsp. celery seed
1/2 tsp. turmeric	

Slice cucumbers and onions into 3 quart bowl and sprinkle each layer with salt. Let stand 2-3 hours and drain. In large kettle, combine vinegar, sugar and spices and bring to boil. Add cucumbers and cook 5 minutes. Pack in jars and seal while hot.
—Nancy Moody Genthner

Bread and Butter Pickles II

4 quarts cucumbers	3 cups vinegar
4 small onions	1 tbsp. white mustard seed
1/2 cup salt	1 tsp. celery seed
1/2 cup sugar	1 tsp. turmeric

Slice cucumbers and onions into bowl and sprinkle with salt. Add water to cover and let stand overnight. Drain. In large saucepan, combine and boil sugar, vinegar and spices. Bring to boil and add cukes and onions. Cook 15 minutes longer. Seal in hot, sterilized jars.
—Thelma Kennedy

Beet Relish

1 quart cooked beets	1 cup sugar
1 quart chopped cabbage	1 tbsp. salt
1/2 cup horseradish	1/2 tsp. black pepper
vinegar	

Chop beets and cabbage fine, as for piccalilli. Combine with remaining ingredients in large kettle and mix with vinegar until consistency of relish. Put in jars and seal. Do not process.
—Nellie Moody Jones

Zucchini Relish

10 cups diced zucchini	2 tsp. turmeric
1 cup pickling salt	1 tbsp. dry mustard
5 cups diced onions	3 tbsp. celery seed
1 cup diced celery	6 cups sugar
3 diced green peppers	5 cups white vinegar
2 diced sweet red peppers	3 tbsp. cornstarch

Combine red and green peppers, onion, celery and zucchini in large bowl and sprinkle with salt. Let stand overnight. Drain vegetables and rinse thoroughly in colander. In large enamelled kettle, combine remaining ingredients with vegetables and bring to a rolling boil. Reduce heat and simmer gently for 20 minutes. Seal in hot, sterilized jars.
—Nellie Moody Jones

Freezer Pickles

2 quarts unpeeled, sliced cucumbers	1 heaping tsp. salt
2 medium onions, thinly sliced	1 1/2 cups sugar
1/2 cup vinegar	

Combine cucumbers, onions and salt in large bowl, and let set 6 hours or more. Boil together sugar and vinegar, and cool in refrigerator until thickened. Drain cucumbers and onions; rinse with cold water. Combine with thickened syrup and pour into freezer containers. Freeze. Ready to use in 5 days.
—Avis Maloney

Ripe Cucumber Pickles

3 quarts peeled, cubed cucumbers	2 cups vinegar
2 large sweet red peppers	3 cups sugar
3 medium onions	3 tbsp. salt
1 tbsp. whole mixed pickling spices, tied in a white cloth	

Peel large, ripe cucumbers, remove seeds, cut and cube. Put peppers and onions through food grinder. Combine cucumbers, onions and red peppers in large kettle and sprinkle with salt. Let stand overnight, or for 3-4 hours. Drain and combine with remaining ingredients in large kettle. Bring to a boil and simmer until cucumbers become transparent and tender. Seal in jars while hot.
—Bertha Moody

Tomato Mincemeat

1 peck green tomatoes, finely chopped	1 cup vinegar
1 peck apples, finely chopped	1 1/2 tbsp. cinnamon
4 lbs. brown sugar	1 1/2 tbsp. cloves
3 cups chopped raisins	1 1/2 tbsp. salt
2 cups chopped suet	1/2 tbsp. nutmeg

Drain chopped tomatoes, cover with cold water and scald three times. Drain. Combine all ingredients in large kettle. Cook 1 hour over low heat, stirring often to prevent sticking. Pour into jars and seal while hot.
—Frances Creamer

Cucumber Relish

4 quarts cucumbers, peeled and cubed

4 large onions	1 tsp. turmeric
2 sweet red peppers	4 tsp. salt
2 green peppers	3 cups sugar
1 tsp. mustard	3 cups vinegar
4 tsp. mustard seed	

Finely chop cucumbers, onions and peppers. Combine with remaining ingredients in large kettle and simmer until vegetables become transparent. Do not boil. Seal in hot, sterilized jars.
—Nellie Moody Jones

Hot Dog Relish

1 sweet red pepper	2 cups green tomatoes
1 green pepper	1/2 cup salt
2 onions	1 1/2 cups sugar
2 cucumbers	1 1/2 cups vinegar
1 handful whole mixed pickling spices, tied in cloth bag	

Chop peppers, tomatoes, cucumbers and onions. Add salt and let stand overnight, or at least 4 hours. Rinse thoroughly in cold water and drain. Combine all ingredients in large kettle and cook 45 minutes over a moderate heat. Seal in hot, sterlized jars.
—Pat Caldwell

—— Soups & Salad ——

Rod McCormick

Moody's Diner 1936

Bubbling Squeak

1 1/4 cups frozen peas	1 lb. ground beef
1 lb. diced potatoes	1 cup chopped onion
1 1/4 cups diced carrots	1 can tomato soup

Cook peas and drain, reserving liquid. Boil potatoes in same water as peas, plus enough water to cover potatoes. When potatoes are nearly cooked, add carrots. Cook ground beef and onions in frying pan. Add tomato soup to cooking vegetables; then stir in cooked beef and onions. Bring to boil, add peas and simmer 5 minutes.
—Thelma Moody

Cheeseburger Chowder

1 lb. ground beef	3 tbsp. flour
1/2 cup finely chopped celery	1/2 tsp. salt
1/4 cup chopped onion	4 cups milk
2 tbsp. chopped green pepper	1 tbsp. beef bouillon
1 cup sharp cheddar cheese, shredded	

Brown ground beef in large skillet or saucepan. Add celery, onion and green pepper. Cook until vegetables are tender. Blend in flour and salt; add milk and bouillon. Cook and stir over low heat until thickened. Add cheese and heat until cheese melts. Serves 4-6.
—Lynne Moody Weister

Hamburger Soup

1 lb. ground beef	1 1/2 qts. water
1 cup chopped potatoes	1 can (28 oz.) crushed tomatoes
1 cup chopped celery	1/4 cup uncooked long-grain rice
1 cup chopped onion	1/2 tsp. basil
1 cup chopped carrots	1/2 tsp. thyme
1 cup chopped cabbage	1 bay leaf
salt and pepper	

Brown ground beef and drain. In large saucepan, combine ground beef with remaining ingredients, except cabbage. Cover and simmer 45 minutes, adding cabbage in last 10 minutes of cooking. Add salt and pepper to taste.
—Peggy Jones

Corn Chowder

1 small piece salt pork, diced	3 tbsp. oleo
1/2 cup chopped onion	1 tsp. salt
2 cups diced potatoes	1 can (10 oz.) creamed corn
2 cups boiling water	1 can (12 oz.) evaporated milk

Saute diced salt pork and chopped onion in oleo. Add water, potatoes and salt. Bring to a boil, and simmer until potatoes are tender. Add creamed corn and evaporated milk. Let chowder sit 30 minutes before serving, to blend flavor.
—Anne Braley

Marge's Mulligatawny Soup

The slower you cook it, the better this soup tastes.

4-5 pieces chicken	1/2 cup chopped celery
1 minced clove garlic	1/2 cup diced onion
2 tbsp. oleo	1/2 cup chopped green pepper
1/2 cup uncooked long-grain rice	1/2 cup chopped cabbage
1 cup sliced carrots	3-4 chicken bouillon cubes

Place chicken in pan and cover with water. Cook chicken until tender; remove chicken from bones and reserve broth. In large saucepan, saute garlic in oleo. Add rice and brown; add carrots, celery, onions and green peppers. Combine 4 cups chicken broth with bouillon cubes and add to vegetables. Add chicken and simmer soup about 1 hour. Add shredded cabbage in last 10 minutes of cooking.
—Nancy Moody Genthner

Margaret's Beef Stew

2 tbsp. melted oleo	1 lb. cubed stew beef
2 tbsp. flour	1 diced onion
1/2 cup catsup	4-5 sliced carrots
3 cups boiling water	3-4 diced potatoes
salt and pepper to taste	

Combine oleo and flour in stew pot or crockpot. Add catsup and boiling water. Add beef, onions and vegetables. Bring to boil and then simmer until beef is tender. In crockpot, simmer all day on Low.
—Mary Olson

Tuna and Broccoli Soup

1/4 cup oleo	1/2 tsp. sage
3 tbsp. minced onion	1/4 tsp. white pepper
3 tbsp. flour	dash cayenne pepper
1 1/4 tsp. salt	4 cups milk
1/2 tsp. celery salt	1 pkg. (10 oz.) frozen broccoli
1 can (6 oz.) tuna, drained and flaked	

Melt oleo in heavy saucepan; add onion and cook until tender. Blend in flour, salt, celery salt, pepper, cayenne pepper and sage. Heat until bubbling; gradually add milk and stir constantly to boiling. Add broccoli and cook over low heat 10-15 minutes, stirring occasionally. Fold in tuna and heat through. Serves 6.
—Hannah Flagg

The inside crew gathered outside for this photograph sometime in the 1940's. They are (left to right) Dewey Moody, Nellie Benner, Clara Barton, Virginia Moody, Elsie Winchenbach, Esther Lovette, Thelma Kennedy, Nellie Moody Jones (standing), Austin Achorn.

Nancy: *Nellie Benner came to take care of Mother after I was born. And then she just stayed.*
Alvah: *One time when the kitchen was just behind the counter, Nellie slipped near the grease kettle. Austin Achorn tried to help her up and he fell down too. There were customers sitting there with the two of them sliding around trying to get up.*

They start young at Moody's Diner.

Aunt Bertha's Salad

1 quart cranberries 3 cups hot water
1 large orange 2 cups sugar
1 large apple 1 pkg. (6 oz.) orange jello
1 can (8 1/2 oz.) crushed pineapple 1 pkg. (6 oz.) mixed fruit jello

Grind together cranberries, orange and apple — including peel. Add pineapple and sugar, and let set 2 hours. Dissolve jello in hot water; add fruit and chill until firm.
—Naomi Walker

Strawberry Salad

2 pkgs. (3 oz.) strawberry jello 1 can (8 1/2 oz.) crushed pineapple
1 pkg. (10 oz.) frozen strawberries 1 cup whole cranberry sauce
2 cups boiling water

Dissolve jello in boiling water. Add strawberries and stir until thawed; add pineapple and cranberry sauce. Refrigerate until firm.
—Nancy Moody Genthner

Roberta's Sinful Salad

1 pkg. (6 oz.) strawberry jello 2 pkgs. (10 oz.) frozen strawberries,
1 cup boiling water thawed and drained
1 cup mashed bananas, about 3 1 can (20 oz.) crushed pineapple, drained
1 cup chopped walnuts 2 cups sour cream

In medium bowl, dissolve jello in boiling water. Cool. Fold in bananas, strawberries, pineapple and walnuts, and stir. Pour half the jello into an 11 x 7 pan and refrigerate until set, about 1 hour. Keep remaining jello at room temperature. Spread sour cream over partially-set jello and cover with remaining jello. Cover and refrigerate until set.
—Judy Moody Beck

Orange-Pineapple Surprise

2 pkgs. (3 oz.) orange OR mixed fruit jello 1 can (20 oz.) crushed pineapple
1 3/4 cups boiling water 3/4 cup diced celery
1 jar (14 oz.) cranberry-orange relish 1/2 cup chopped walnuts OR pecans

Dissolve jello in boiling water; add relish and mix well. Stir in pineapple, celery and nuts. Pour into 6-cup mold. Chill until firm and unmold on lettuce-lined plate. Serve with mayonnaise dressing, if desired.
—Joan Moody

Martian Salad

1 box instant pistachio pudding   2 cups miniature marshmallows
1 can (6 oz.) pineapple chunks   1/4 cup chopped nuts, optional
1 container cool whip

Pour pudding mix into bowl; add pineapple and juice. Add remaining ingredients and stir well. Refrigerate several hours before serving.
—Chris Reed

Mom's May Day Salad

2 cups cottage cheese   2 1/2 cups crushed pineapple
1 container cool whip   1 pkg. (3 oz.) lime jello
2 cups fruit cocktail   1 pkg. (3 oz.) lemon jello
1/2 cup chopped nuts

Mix cottage cheese with dry jello; add drained fruit and nuts. Fold in cool whip. Any combination of fruits and jello can be used.
—Judy Moody Beck

Green Molded Salad

1 pkg. (3 oz.) lime jello   1 pkg. (8 oz.) cream cheese, softened
1 cup boiling water   1 1/2 cups miniature marshmallows
1/2 cup cold water   1 2/3 cups crushed pineapple
1/2 cup chopped nuts, optional

Dissolve jello in boiling water, then add cold water. Mix cream cheese into jello, using an egg beater. Chill 1 1/2-2 hours. Fold in marshmallows, pineapple and nuts. Pour into mold and refrigerate until firm.
—Janet Braley

Fruit Salad

1 can (16 oz.) fruit cocktail   1 cup miniature marshmallows
1 can (6 oz.) pineapple chunks   1 cup sour cream
1 can (6 oz.) mandarin oranges   1/4 cup nuts or shredded coconut, optional

Drain all fruit, and mix with marshmallows and sour cream. Let set in refrigerator overnight before serving.
—Jan Jones

Lemon-Ginger Chicken Salad

1/2 cup mayonnaise	1/2 tsp. ground ginger
1/4 cup sour cream	1/2 tsp. curry powder
1 tbsp. sugar	2 cups cubed chicken
1/2 tsp. lemon rind	1 cup green grapes
1 tbsp. lemon juice	1 cup sliced celery
	1/4 cup toasted almonds

In large bowl, mix together mayonnaise, sour cream, sugar, lemon rind, lemon juice, ginger and curry powder. Fold in chicken, grapes and celery. Toss to coat. Chill before serving. Serve on cantaloupe halves and sprinkle with toasted almonds.
—Dorothy Bruns Moody

Seven Layer Salad

1 head iceberg lettuce, shredded	1/2 cup sharp Cheddar cheese, shredded
1 cup diced green pepper	1/2 cup crisp bacon bits
1 cup chopped celery	2 tbsp. brown sugar
1 lg. chopped onion	2 cups mayonnaise
	1 can (16 oz.) drained peas, optional

In large salad bowl, layer each ingredient as listed above. Do not toss. Cover and refrigerate at least 8 hours before serving.
—Chris Reed

Grammie Buck's Potato Salad

12-15 large potatoes	1 tbsp. celery salt
10 hard-boiled eggs	1 1/2 tbsp. onion powder
4 cups mayonnaise	salt and pepper to taste
	parsley OR paprika for garnish

Peel and boil potatoes until tender. Drain and mash while still hot. Dice 9 boiled eggs and combine with hot potatoes. Add mayonnaise, celery salt, onion powder, salt and pepper, and mix well. Grate remaining egg over top of salad. Garnish with parsley or paprika.
—Anne Braley

Potato Salad

4 cups cubed, cooked potatoes	1/2 cup mayonnaise OR salad dressing
1/4 cup oil	1 cup diced celery
2 tbsp. vinegar	2-3 tbsp. chopped onion
3 chopped hard-boiled eggs	salt and pepper to taste

Marinate potatoes 1-2 hours in oil and vinegar. Add remaining ingredients and mix well. Season with salt and pepper. Garnish with parsley or hard-boiled egg and serve in lettuce-lined bowl.
—Hannah Flagg

Mexican Taco Salad

1/2 lb. ground beef,   2 med. chopped tomatoes
browned and drained   1 head shredded lettuce
1 can (12 oz.) kidney beans,   1 cup shredded cheddar cheese
drained and rinsed   1 pkg. crushed taco chips
1 small chopped onion

Combine all ingredients and mix well. Top with 1/3 cup Catalina dressing. Serves 8-10.
—Linda Moody Davis

Salad Dressing

2 eggs   1 tsp. salt
1 tbsp. dry mustard   1 cup vinegar
1 tsp. white pepper   1/2 cup melted oleo
1 can (12 oz.) condensed milk

Beat together eggs, mustard and pepper. Add melted oleo, condensed milk, vinegar and salt. Mix well.
—Corinne Perkins

Lorraine's Barbecue Sauce

2 cups catsup   1 tbsp. onion powder
1 tsp. pepper   1 1/2 cups vinegar
1/2-3/4 cup sugar   8 tsp. Worcestershire sauce

Combine all ingredients in saucepan and simmer 10-15 minutes.
—Rebecca Little

P.B. Moody learned his marketing skills early in life. Here he is (boy on far right) with his family promoting the vacation rooms they used to let each summer.

—— Bread & Muffins ——

Apricot-Oatmeal Muffins

1 egg	1 tsp. salt
1 cup buttermilk	1 tsp. baking powder
1/2 cup brown sugar	1/2 tsp. baking soda
1/3 cup shortening	1 cup dry oatmeal
1 cup flour	1/2 cup dried apricots, chopped

In large bowl, beat egg, buttermilk, brown sugar and shortening. Sift all dry ingredients, except oatmeal, and add to batter. Mix thoroughly. Fold in apricots and oatmeal, and stir until moistened. Spoon batter into 12 greased muffin cups, 2/3 full. Bake 15-20 minutes at 400 degrees.
—Dorothy Bruns Moody

Blueberry Muffins

1/4 cup oleo	2 cups flour
1/2 cup sugar	3 tsp. baking powder
1 egg	1/2 tsp. salt
1 cup milk	1 1/2 cups blueberries

Cream together oleo and sugar; add egg and beat well. Mix in dry ingredients, then stir in milk. Dust blueberries with flour and fold into batter. Spoon into 12 greased muffin tins, 2/3 full, and bake 25 minutes at 350 degrees.
—Nancy Moody Genthner

Molasses Bran Muffins

This batter makes a very moist bran muffin.

1 cup all-bran	1 cup flour
1 cup dry oatmeal	1 tsp. baking soda
1 1/2 cups milk	1 tsp. salt
1 egg	1/2 cup molasses

Mix bran and oatmeal with milk and let set until soft. When soft, stir in egg and molasses, then add dry ingredients. Pour batter into greased muffin tins, 2/3 full, and bake 15- 20 minutes at 350 degrees.
—Nancy Moody Genthner

Doughnut Muffins

1 egg	2 tsp. baking powder
1/3 cup oil	1/2 tsp. salt
1/2 cup milk	1/2 tsp. nutmeg
1 1/2 cups flour	1/2 cup sugar

Beat egg in large bowl; add oil and milk and beat again. Sift dry ingredients and stir into batter. Pour batter, half-filling, 12 greased muffin tins. Top each muffin with pat of oleo and dash of cinnamon sugar. Bake 20 minutes at 400 degrees.
—Nancy Little

Mom's Molasses Doughnuts

2 eggs	3/4 tsp. salt
3/4 cup sugar	1/2 tsp. cinnamon
1/2 cup molasses	1 tsp. nutmeg
2 tbsp. melted shortening	3 1/2 cups flour
1 cup buttermilk OR sour milk	1 rounded tsp. baking soda
	1/4 tsp. ginger

Beat eggs until light; add sugar and beat well. Add molasses, shortening and buttermilk. Sift dry ingredients and add to batter. Chill several hours before frying dough in hot fat.
—Nellie Moody Jones

Grammy's Chocolate Doughnuts

dash of salt	2 eggs
3 1/2 cups flour	1 tsp. vanilla
1 1/4 cups sugar	pinch of ginger
3 heaping tbsp. cocoa	3 tbsp. melted shortening
1 heaping tsp. baking soda	1 cup buttermilk OR sour milk

Sift together dry ingredients except sugar and set aside. Beat eggs in large bowl; add sugar, melted shortening, buttermilk and vanilla. Mix thoroughly. Stir in dry ingredients and mix. Do not overmix. Let batter rest 30 minutes. On floured surface, roll out dough to 1/2-inch thickness. Cut with doughnut cutter and fry in hot fat. To make plain doughnuts, omit cocoa and add 1 tsp. nutmeg.
—Pat Caldwell

Mom's Brown Bread

1 cup rolled oats	1/2 tsp. salt
3 cups graham flour	1 cup molasses
3 cups buttermilk OR sour milk	3 tsp. baking soda

Combine all ingredients in large bowl, and mix well. Pour batter into greased coffee cans, 2/3 full. Cover top with tin foil and steam 3 hours. Makes four 1 lb. loaves.
—Debbie Moody Bellows

Brown Bread

1 cup graham flour 1 cup molasses
1 cup cornmeal 2 cups buttermilk OR sour milk
1 cup white flour 1 1/2 tsp. baking soda
1 tsp. salt

Combine dry ingredients. Add buttermilk and molasses, and mix thoroughly. Pour batter into two well-greased 1 lb. coffee cans. Cover with wax paper and secure with elastic band. Steam 2 hours.
—Anne Braley

Best-Ever Banana Bread

1 cup sugar 2 cups flour
1/2 cup oleo 1 tsp. baking powder
2 beaten eggs 1/2 tsp. salt
1 cup mashed bananas 1/4 cup buttermilk OR sour milk
1/2 cup chopped nuts

Cream together oleo and sugar; add eggs and banana, and mix well. Combine dry ingredients and add to batter, alternately with buttermilk. Fold in nuts. Bake in 8 x 4 loaf pan 1 hour at 350 degrees.
—Judy Moody Beck

Patrick Downs

Peg's Pumpkin Bread

1 3/4 cups flour	1/2 tsp. nutmeg
1/4 tsp. baking powder	1 1/2 cups sugar
1 tsp. baking soda	1/2 cup oil
1 tsp. salt	2 eggs
1/2 tsp. cloves	1 cup cooked pumpkin
1/2 tsp. cinnamon	1/3 cup water
1/2 tsp. allspice	

Sift together dry ingredients, except sugar. In large bowl, combine sugar and oil. Add eggs and pumpkin, and beat thoroughly. Stir in dry ingredients and water. Mix well and pour batter into a greased and floured loaf pan. Bake 1 hour at 350 degrees.
—Nancy Moody Genthner

Newfoundland-Avondale
Rhubarb Bread

2 1/4 cups sifted flour	1/2 tsp. allspice
1 cup whole wheat flour	3 eggs
2 tsp. baking soda	1 cup oil
1 tsp. baking powder	1 3/4 cups packed brown sugar
1 tsp. salt	2 tsp. vanilla
2 tsp. cinnamon	2 1/2 cups chopped rhubarb
1/2 tsp. nutmeg	3/4 cup chopped walnuts

Combine first 8 ingredients and set aside. In large bowl, beat eggs, oil, brown sugar and vanilla with electric mixer at high speed until fluffy and smooth — about 5 minutes. Stir in dry ingredients then fold in rhubarb and nuts. Pour batter in two greased loaf pans and bake 1 hour at 350 degrees. Dust with powdered sugar when cool.
—Debbie Moody Bellows

Rhubarb Bread

2 3/4 cups flour	1/2 cup oil
1 1/2 cups packed brown sugar	1 tsp. vanilla
1 tsp. baking soda	1 cup chopped rhubarb
1 tsp. salt	2 tbsp. flour
1 egg	2-3 tsp. oleo
1 cup buttermilk	2-3 tsp. granulated sugar

Toss rhubarb with 2 tbsp. flour and set aside. In large bowl, stir together flour, brown sugar, baking soda and salt. In separate bowl, combine egg, buttermilk, oil and vanilla. Mix well and stir in dry ingredients. Fold rhubarb into batter and pour into two greased 8 x 4 loaf pans. Top each loaf with pats of oleo and sprinkle with sugar. Bake 55 minutes at 350 degrees.
—Gail Kennedy

Strawberry Bread

4 beaten eggs	1 tsp. baking soda
1 1/2 cups oil	1 tsp. salt
2 cups sugar	1 tbsp. cinnamon
3 cups flour	1 1/2 cups chopped walnuts

2 cups fresh OR frozen strawberries, sliced

Sift dry ingredients and set aside. In large bowl, beat together eggs, oil and sugar. Add dry ingredients and mix well. Fold in strawberries and nuts, and pour into two greased loaf pans. Bake 1 hour at 350 degrees.
—Judy Moody Beck

Zucchini Bread

3 eggs	3 cups flour
1 cup oil	2 tsp. baking soda
2 cups sugar	1 tsp. salt
2 tsp. vanilla	1/2 tsp. baking powder
2 cups coarsely shredded zucchini	1 1/2 tsp. cinnamon
1 can (8 1/2 oz.) crushed pineapple, drained	3/4 tsp. nutmeg
	1 cup nuts, raisins or dates, optional

Beat eggs in large bowl and add oil, sugar and vanilla. Beat until thick and foamy. Stir in zucchini and pineapple. Sift and add dry ingredients until just blended. Fold in nuts or raisins and pour batter into two 5 x 9 greased loaf pans. Bake 1 hour at 350 degrees.
—Jean Moody

Zucchini-Orange Bread

4 eggs	1 1/2 tsp. baking powder
1 1/2 cups sugar	1 tsp. salt
3/4 cup oil	2 tsp. grated orange peel
2/3 cup orange juice	2 1/2 tsp. cinnamon
2 cups shredded zucchini	1/2 tsp. cloves
3 1/4 cups flour	1/2 cup chopped nuts

In large bowl, mix together eggs and sugar. Add oil and orange juice, and mix well. Sift dry ingredients and add to egg batter. Stir thoroughly and fold in zucchini and nuts. Pour batter into two, greased and floured loaf pans. Bake 45-55 minutes at 350 degrees.
When cooled, top this bread with a glaze of 1 cup powdered sugar combined with 2-3 tbsp. orange juce.
—Mary Olson

Chocolate Zucchini Bread

3 eggs	2 1/2 cups flour
3/4 cup melted oleo	1 tsp. cinnamon
2 cups sugar	2 1/2 tsp. baking powder
2 tsp. vanilla	1/2 cup cocoa
3 tsp. grated orange peel	1 1/2 tsp. baking soda
	2 cups grated zucchini

In large bowl, beat eggs; add sugar and melted oleo. Add vanilla and beat well. Sift dry ingredients and stir into egg mixture. Fold in zucchini and orange rind and pour batter into two greased and floured loaf pans. Bake 40-45 minutes at 350 degrees.
—Irene Duprey

Blueberry Crumb Coffee Cake

2 cups flour	1/2 cup shortening
1/2 tsp. salt	1 beaten egg
3 tsp. baking powder	1/2 cup milk
1/2 cup sugar	2 tsp. lemon juice
	2 cups blueberries

Crumb Topping:

1/3 cup sugar	1/2 tsp. cinnamon
1/3 cup flour	1/4 cup oleo

Sift flour, salt and baking powder and set aside. In large bowl, cream shortening and sugar; add egg and beat until light. Stir milk into eggs, alternating with dry ingredients. Mix well and pour batter into 8-inch greased loaf pan lined with wax paper. Pour lemon juice over blueberries and spread over batter. In small bowl, combine sugar, flour and cinnamon. Add oleo and mix until small crumbs form. Sprinkle topping over blueberries. Bake 55-60 minutes at 350 degrees. Serve warm.
—Gail Kennedy

Cranberry Coffee Cake

1/2 cup oleo	2 cups flour
1 cup sugar	1/2 tsp. salt
2 eggs	1 cup sour cream
1 tsp. baking powder	1 tsp. almond extract
1 tsp. baking soda	1 can (16 oz.) whole cranberry sauce
1/2 cup chopped walnuts	

In large bowl, cream oleo and sugar; add eggs and beat well. Add dry ingredients alternately with almond flavoring and sour cream and mix thoroughly. Spread half the batter in greased, 9-inch tube pan and top with half the cranberry sauce. Add remaining batter and top with remaining sauce. Sprinkle with nuts and bake 55 minutes at 350 degrees.
—Nellie Moody Jones

Prune-Apricot Coffee Cake

3/4 cup sugar	3/4 cup chopped apricots
3/4 cup softened shortening	2 cups flour
2 eggs	2 tsp. baking powder
3/4 cup chopped prunes	3/4 cup milk
1 tsp. vanilla	

Topping:

2/3 cup packed brown sugar	1 tbsp. cinnamon
1 tbsp. flour	1/2 cup chopped nuts
6 tbsp. melted oleo	

Let prunes and apricots stand in hot water 5 minutes. Drain. In large bowl, cream sugar and shortening; add eggs and mix well. Add dry ingredients alternately with milk and vanilla. Stir and fold in prunes and apricots. Pour 1/3 of the batter into greased and floured tube pan; cover with 1/3 of the topping. Sprinkle with 1/3 of the nuts and melted oleo. Repeat layers. Bake 55 minutes at 350 degrees.
—Ona Moody

Mom's Biscuits

4 cups flour	1/2 tsp. salt
2 tbsp. baking powder	2 cups milk
1/4 cup shortening	

Sift together dry ingredients. Cut shortening into dry ingredients until mixture resembles fine meal. Add milk and stir with fork. Turn dough onto floured surface and knead enough to roll. Cut with biscuit cutter, place on pan and bake at 500 degrees until browned on top.
—Nellie Moody Jones

Oatmeal Bread

1/2 cup warm water	1/2 cup molasses
1 yeast cake OR 2 oz. pkg. active dry yeast	2 tsp. salt
2 cups scalded milk	1 tbsp. shortening
1 cup oatmeal	4 1/2-5 cups flour

Mix water with yeast and set aside. Allow milk to cool, then mix with oatmeal, molasses, salt, shortening and yeast. Add flour until dough is easy to handle. Add more flour as necessary. Turn dough onto floured surface and knead 3-4 minutes. Place in greased bowl to rise until doubled in volume. Knead again and divide dough. Shape into loaves or place in two greased loaf pans and let rise again. Bake loaves 20-30 minutes at 350 degrees. Brush tops of loaves with butter after cooking.
—Susan Moody

Oatmeal Bread II

1 cup rolled oats	2 tsp. salt
2 cups boiling water	2 tbsp. softened oleo
2 pkgs. active dry yeast	1/2 cup molasses
1/3 cup lukewarm water	5 1/2 - 6 cups flour

Put oats in large bowl and cover with boiling water. Let stand 30 minutes (water should still be warm). Sprinkle yeast into lukewarm water and let stand 5 minutes (do not stir). Meanwhile, add salt, oleo and molasses to soaked oats. Stir yeast and pour into oats. Stir in 2 cups flour, then add 3-4 cups more. (Work in the last of the flour by hand.) Knead dough on floured surface and place in greased bowl to rise until doubled in bulk (about 2 hours). Punch down dough and divide. Shape into loaves and place in well-greased loaf pans. Cover and let rise 1 hour. Bake 50 minutes at 350 degrees.
—Chris Reed

Oatmeal Bread III

A very moist bread.

1 1/2 cups boiling water	1 tsp. salt
1 cup quick-cooking oats	2 yeast cakes
1/3 cup softened shortening	1/2 cup warm water
1/2 cup molasses	2 beaten eggs
5 1/2 cups flour	

Combine boiling water, oats, shortening, salt and molasses. Stir and cool. Dissolve yeast cakes in warm water and add to oats. Mix well. Blend in beaten eggs and add flour. Turn dough onto floured surface and knead. Place in greased bowl and let rise until doubled in volume. Punch down dough and knead again. Divide dough, place in two greased loaf pans and let rise again. Bake 35 minutes at 375 degrees.
—Judy Moody Beck

Coffee Bread

2 pkgs. active dry yeast	1/2 cup oleo
1/2 cup lukewarm water	1 tsp. vanilla
4 beaten eggs	22 cardamom seeds, finely pounded OR
1 cup sugar	1 tbsp. ground cardamom
2 cups scalded milk	7 cups flour

Dissolve yeast in warm water. Add oleo to scalded milk. In large bowl, beat eggs and sugar until spongy; add vanilla and cardamom. Mix well, and add yeast and milk. Stir in enough flour to make dough easy to handle. Turn dough onto floured surface and knead. Place in warmed, greased bowl and let rise until doubled in bulk. Divide dough into three equal parts to make three loaves. Divide dough again and braid. Place braided loaves on greased baking sheet to rise. Bake 20 minutes at 350 degrees.
—Marion A. Whitmore

Nissua
Finnish Bread

3/4 cup oleo	3 pkgs. active dry yeast
3/4 cup sugar	1 cup warm water
2 tsp. salt	9-10 crushed cardamom seeds
2 cups scalded milk	6 beaten eggs
10-11 cups flour	

Stir oleo, sugar and salt into scalded milk, and set aside to cool. In small bowl, dissolve yeast in warm water. When milk is lukewarm, add crushed cardamom seeds, dissolved yeast and beaten eggs. Stir in 6 cups of flour and knead about 10 minutes. Knead in remaining flour and let rise until doubled in bulk (about 1 1/2 hours). Punch down and let dough rise 30 minutes more. Punch down again and divide into four equal lengths and braid to make 4 loaves. Let rise 1 hour. Beat 1 egg and brush on loaves, then sprinkle with sugar. Bake 20 minutes at 350 degrees. Decorate for the holidays with powdered sugar icing, red and green glace cherries and walnuts. Omit brushed egg.
—Dot Aho Moody

Irish Freckle Bread

1 small potato, pared	1/2 cup sugar
1 cup raisins	1/2 cup melted oleo
2 pkgs. active dry yeast	4 1/2 cups flour
1/2 cup very warm water	1 tsp. salt
2 beaten eggs	1/2 tsp. cinnamon

Cook potato in 1 cup water for 15 minutes. Leave potato in water and mash. Measure and add water, if necessary, to make 1 cup potato. Stir raisins into potato and let cool. In large bowl, sprinkle yeast into very warm water, and stir until yeast is dissolved. Add mashed potato and raisins. Mix in beaten eggs, sugar and melted oleo. Stir in 2 cups flour, salt and cinnamon and mix until batter is smooth. Stir in remaining flour to make stiff dough. Turn out on floured surface and knead dough until smooth and elastic. Place in large greased bowl, turning to coat with shortening. Cover bowl with cloth and let dough rise until doubled in size. Punch down and knead several times. Divide dough and shape into loaves. Place in two greased loaf pans and let rise 45 minutes. Bake 35 minutes at 350 degrees, until golden brown and loaves make a hollow sound when tapped. Brush with glaze.

Freckle Bread Glaze: 1/2 cup light corn syrup and 1/2 cup water, heated to boiling and simmered 5 minutes. Remove from heat and stir in 1/2 tsp. vanilla. Brush generously onto each loaf.
—Andrea Newbert

Dark Yeast Rolls

1/2 cup shortening	2 tbsp. brown sugar
1/2 cup rolled oats	1 1/2 cups boiling water and milk, combined
1/2 cup all-bran	2 pkgs. active dry yeast
1 tsp. salt	1/3 cup lukewarm water
3 tbsp. molasses	4 cups flour

In large bowl, mix shortening, oats, bran, salt, molasses and sugar. Cover with combined boiling water-milk, and cool until lukewarm. Dissolve yeast in lukewarm water and add to oats. Stir. Add flour and mix well. Cover and let dough rise until doubled in bulk. Turn dough onto floured surface; knead and shape into rolls. Place on greased baking sheets and let rise again. Bake 20 minutes at 400 degrees.
—Nancy Moody Genthner

Refrigerator Rolls

2 cups boiling water	2 yeast cakes OR pkgs. active dry yeast
1/2 cup shortening	1 tsp. sugar
1/2 cup sugar	1/4 cup lukewarm water
1 tsp. salt	2 eggs, lightly beaten
8 cups sifted flour	

Mix boiling water, shortening, sugar and salt in large bowl, and stir until shortening melts. Dissolve yeast in lukewarm water and add sugar. When shortening and water mix is lukewarm, stir in yeast. Add eggs and 4 cups flour. Beat thoroughly and add remaining flour. Mix, but do not knead; the dough should be soft. Cover and store in refrigerator. To bake, remove dough from refrigerator, shape into rolls and let rise until doubled in bulk. Bake 15-20 minutes at 400 degrees.
—Doris Moody Eaton

Sixty-Minute Rolls

2 pkgs. active dry yeast	3 1/2 - 4 1/2 cups sifted flour
1/4 cup lukewarm water	3/4 tsp. salt
1 1/4 cups milk	1/4 cup oleo
3 tbsp. sugar	

Dissolve yeast in lukewarm water. Combine milk, sugar, salt and half the oleo in small saucepan and heat until lukewarm. Add yeast, mix well and stir in flour. Cover dough and let rise in warm place 15 minutes. Turn dough onto floured surface and pat to 1/2-inch thickness. Cut with 2-inch biscuit cutter and place on greased baking sheet. Brush with remaining oleo and fold dough in half. Let rise 15 minutes more. Bake 10 minutes at 400 degrees.
—Nancy Moody Genthner

Cherry Peek-a-Boo Rolls

2 pkgs. active dry yeast	2 tsp. salt
1/2 cup lukewarm water	2 eggs
1 1/4 cups scalded milk	7-7 1/2 cups sifted flour
1/2 cup sugar	4 tbsp. oleo
6 tbsp. oleo	1 jar cherry preserves

Dissolve yeast in lukewarm water and set aside. Combine scalded milk and sugar with oleo and salt. Stir. Add dissolved yeast, eggs and 2 cups flour, and beat until smooth. Add 5-5 1/2 cups flour, to make a soft dough. Turn dough onto floured surface and knead until smooth and satiny. Place dough in greased bowl and turn once. Cover and let rise until doubled in bulk (about 1 1/2 hours). Punch down and roll out dough 1/2-inch thick on lightly floured surface. Spread dough with soft oleo and fold in half. Pinch edges together and again roll dough 1/2-inch thick. Brush with oleo, fold in half and roll 1/2-inch thick. Cut in 2 1/2-inch circles and place on greased cookie sheet. Cover and let rise 30 minutes. Depress center of each circle and fill with cherry preserves. Bake 15 minutes at 400 degrees. Frost with powdered sugar icing and decorate with slivered almonds.
—Pat Caldwell

Patrick Downs

—— Main Course Dishes ——

Rod McCormick

Moody's Diner 1938

Curried Chicken Divan

1 pkg. (10 oz.) frozen broccoli, cooked — 3/4 cup grated Cheddar cheese
3 chicken breasts, cooked and cubed — 1 can (10 oz.) cream of chicken soup
1/2 cup mayonnaise — 1/4-1/2 tsp. curry powder
1 tsp. lemon juice — 1/4 tsp. paprika

Place cooked broccoli in greased baking dish and cover with chicken. Combine remaining ingredients, reserving half the cheese, and pour over chicken. Top with remaining cheese and shake paprika on top. Bake uncovered 25-30 minutes at 350 degrees.
—Cathy Sprague

Chicken Divan

3 chicken breasts — 1/2 cup chicken broth
2 pkgs. (10 oz.) frozen broccoli spears — 1 can (10 oz.) cream of chicken soup
1/2 cup mayonnaise — 1 cup sour cream
1/4 tsp. paprika — 1/2 cup grated parmesan cheese

Boil chicken until tender; remove meat from bone and cut into bite-size pieces. Partially cook broccoli (about 5 minutes). Arrange chicken in a well-greased, 12 x 8 baking dish and cover with broccoli. Blend broth, soup, mayonnaise and sour cream, and pour over chicken and broccoli. Top with cheese and paprika, and bake 25-30 minutes at 350 degrees.
—Chris Reed

Who are those young fella's? The above picture of Alvah Moody and Bill Jones was taken in the early 1950's as a publicity shot for the company that installed the stainless steel work. Moody's kitchen was one of their first.

Alvah Moody   Bill Jones

Marian Savage

49

Chicken Gumbo

4 chicken breasts   1/2 bag seasoned breadcrumbs
2 cans (10 oz.) cream of chicken soup   1 can (10 oz.) cream of mushroom soup
1 3/4 cups milk   1 can (4 oz.) mushrooms

Cook chicken until tender; remove from bone and cube. Place pieces in a 9 x 13 baking pan. Heat cream of chicken soup with milk and pour over chicken. Top with breadcrumbs. Bake at 325 degrees until hot. Combine and cook undrained mushrooms, mushroom soup and 1/2 cup of milk. Pour over chicken and serve.
—Norma Moody Dion

Chicken and Mushrooms in Orange Sauce

1 chicken, cut into serving size pieces OR 3 large split chicken breasts
1/2-3/4 lb. fresh mushrooms   1 cup orange juice
1 sliced green pepper   1/2 cup water
1 sliced yellow onion   1/4 cup white wine
2 rounded tbsp. cornstarch
1 tbsp. frozen orange juice concentrate, optional
grated orange peel, optional

Lightly salt chicken and broil, skin side up, for 10 minutes. Slice vegetables and spread in bottom of large baking dish. Combine orange juice, water and wine with cornstarch, and cook over low heat until sauce thickens. For a stronger orange flavor add 1 tbsp. frozen orange juice concentrate. Cover vegetables with chicken and top with sauce. Bake 1 hour at 350 degrees, until chicken is tender. Sprinkle with grated orange peel for extra flavor and garnish.
—Clara Moody Kiener

Lemon Chicken

1/3 cup flour   1 chicken bouillon cube
1 tsp. salt   3 tbsp. oil
1 tsp. paprika   3/4 cup water
3 lb. frying chicken   2 tbsp. brown sugar
3 tbsp. lemon juice   1/4 cup sliced green onion
1 1/2 tsp. grated lemon peel, optional

In a bag, combine flour, salt and paprika. Cut chicken into pieces and brush with lemon juice. Place chicken, two pieces at a time, into bag and shake well. Heat oil in large skillet and brown chicken. Dissolve bouillon cube in 3/4 cup boiling water and pour over chicken. Stir in onion, brown sugar, lemon peel and remaining lemon juice. Cook over low heat until tender, about 45 minutes.
—Peggy Jones

Sticky Chicken

1/2 cup sugar   1/2 cup soy sauce
1/2 cup vinegar   1 chicken, cut into pieces

Mix and heat sugar, vinegar and soy sauce in deep skillet. Add chicken and cook over moderate heat for 20 minutes, occasionally turning chicken. Cover and cook another 10 minutes. Remove cover and allow sauce to thicken and coat chicken, about 10 minutes. Then serve. Chicken can be marinated overnight before cooking.
—Naomi Walker

Quick Stir-Fried Chicken

3 tbsp. peanut oil   2 cups raw chicken,
4 tbsp. soy sauce   sliced julienne
3/4 tsp. garlic salt   2 oranges, sectioned
2 tsp. cornstarch   2 cups cooked rice OR
3 tbsp. cold water   chow mein noodles
1 pkg. (6 oz.) frozen, Chinese peapods   1 bunch green onions, trimmed and quartered
1/2 cup sliced mushrooms   3/4 cup chopped fresh broccoli
1 can (8 oz.) water chestnuts, drained and sliced

Heat oil in wok or skillet over medium heat. When hot, add soy sauce and garlic salt, and stir. Combine cornstarch and water, and set aside. Add chicken to pan and stir-fry, about 3 minutes. Add peapods, water chestnuts and broccoli, and stir-fry 2 minutes. Reduce heat then add orange sections, green onions, mushrooms and cornstarch. Stir until thickened and serve over rice or noodles.
—Shawn M. Moody

Sweet and Sour Chicken

4-6 pieces chicken   2 tbsp. soy sauce
2/3 cup sugar   1 tbsp. oil
1/4 cup catsup   1 tsp. garlic powder
1/2 cup pineapple juice   2 tbsp. cornstarch
1/2 cup white vinegar   1/2 cup cold water
1 cup pineapple chunks

Cook chicken and set aside. In medium saucepan, combine all ingredients except cornstarch, water andpineapple chunks. Heat to boiling. Add cornstarch mixed with water, then add pineapple chunks. Remove from heat and add chicken. Let stand a few minutes before serving over cooked rice.
This is very good when prepared ahead and marinated overnight. Just reheat before serving.
—Gail Kennedy

Ground Turkey Loaf

1 lb. ground turkey	1 chopped onion
1 egg	3 slices soft wheat bread
1 pkg. onion soup mix	1/2 cup bran
1 can (4 oz.) mushrooms, drained	1/4 cup dry oat bran cereal
barbecue sauce	

Combine all ingredients except barbecue sauce, and shape into a loaf. Place in loaf pan and top with barbecue sauce. Bake 1 1/2 hours at 325 degrees.
—Shawn M. Moody

Turkey and Broccoli Quiche

2 cups turkey, cooked and cubed	1 cup shredded Cheddar cheese
1/3 cup finely chopped onion	2 cups cooked broccoli
1 unbaked 9-inch pie shell	4 eggs
2 cups milk	3/4 tsp. salt

Spread turkey, cheese, onion and broccoli in pie shell. Beat eggs slightly, then beat in remaining ingredients. Pour into pie shell and bake 15 minutes at 425 degrees. Reduce oven to 300 and bake another 30 minutes, or until knife comes out clean when inserted in center of quiche. Let stand 10 minutes before serving.
—Sheri Beck

American Lasagne

1 lb. ground beef	3/4 tsp. pepper
2 cloves chopped garlic	1/2 tsp. oregano
1 can (6 oz.) tomato paste	1 pkg. (8-oz.) lasagne noodles
2 1/2 cups canned tomatoes	8 oz. Swiss OR mozarella cheese
1 tsp. salt	12 oz. cottage cheese

Brown ground beef and garlic in skillet. Add tomato paste, tomatoes and spices, cover and simmer 20 minutes. Half-cook noodles and drain. Coat bottom of 12 x 9 baking dish with thin layer of sauce. In baking dish, alternate layers of cooked noodles with cheeses and meat sauce. Bake 20-30 minutes at 350 degrees.
—Jean Moody

Crockpot Mock Lasagne

1 pkg. (10 oz.) lasagne noodles	12 oz. cottage cheese
1 lb. ground beef	1 1/2 tbsp. parsley
1 chopped onion	1 jar (32 oz.) spaghetti sauce
12 oz. mozarella cheese	2 tbsp. grated parmesan cheese
1/2 lb. Italian sausage, optional	

Break noodles into bite-size pieces, cook and drain. Brown meat and drain. Grease crock pot. Combine all ingredients in crock pot and stir lightly. Top with grated parmesan cheese and cook 7-9 hours on Low or 3-5 hours on High.
—Cynthia Hilton

Vegetable Lasagne

2 tbsp. olive oil	2 cups shredded Cheddar cheese
1 large chopped onion	1 egg
1 minced garlic clove	1 jar (32-oz.) spaghetti sauce
1 tsp. Italian seasoning	1/2 cup water
2 pkgs. (10-oz.) chopped broccoli,	2 tbsp. vinegar
thawed and drained	9 cooked lasagne noodles
1 can (10 oz.) cream of mushroom soup	2 cups shredded mozarella cheese

Saute onion, garlic and seasonings in oil until transparent. Stir in broccoli and cook until tender. Remove from heat and stir in soup, Cheddar cheese and egg. Set aside. In a medium bowl, stir together sauce, water and vinegar. Pour half the sauce into 13 x 9 baking dish. Alternate layers of noodles, filling and remaining sauce. Bake 40 minutes at 350 degrees. Sprinkle remaining mozarella on top and bake 5 more minutes. Let stand 15 minutes before serving.
—Chris Reed

Pizzasagne

1 pkg. (8 oz.) lasagne noodles	1 lb. cottage cheese
1 jar (32-oz.) spaghetti sauce	1 cup (8 oz.) shredded mozzarella cheese
pinch of oregano	2 oz. thinly sliced pepperoni

Cook and drain lasagne. Spread 1 cup spaghetti sauce in 9 x 13 baking dish. Top with layer of noodles, sauce, a dash of oregano, cottage cheese and mozarella. Repeat layers and top with mozarella and pepperoni. Bake 30-40 minutes at 350 degrees, until bubbling. Remove from oven and let stand 15 minutes before serving.
—Jolene Millay

Pesto and Basil Spaghetti Sauce

3 cups fresh basil leaves	1/2 cup olive oil
2-4 cloves garlic	1/4 cup melted oleo
1/2 cup nuts	salt to taste
3/4 cup chopped fresh parsley	3/4 cup grated parmesan cheese
juice of 1/2 lemon	

Combine all ingredients in food processor and zing into a smooth paste. Serve sauce uncooked over pasta. It is potent and delicious. Pine nuts, sunflower seeds, walnuts or almonds can be used in this recipe.
—Brian Moody

Braised Short Ribs

4 lbs. short ribs (pork or beef)	1/2 cup catsup or tomato paste
2 tsp. salt	1/4 cup water
1/4 tsp. pepper	1/4 cup vinegar
1 tsp. dry mustard	1 tbsp. brown sugar
1 tbsp. soy sauce	1 medium chopped onion
2 cloves minced garlic	

Cut ribs into serving portions, figuring 3/4-1 lb. per person. In a dutch oven or large skillet, brown ribs on both sides over high heat. Drain meat and set aside. Combine remaining ingredients and spoon over, around and under ribs. Bake covered for 2 hours at 350 degrees.
—Rayetta Flint

Oven Beef or Venison Stew

2 lbs. beef or venison	1 cup tomato juice
1/2 cup chopped celery	2 tbsp. tapioca
5 small whole onions	1 tbsp. sugar
7 medium sliced carrots	2 tsp. salt, optional
4 large cubed potatoes	1 handful fresh, chopped parsley

Cut meat into cubes. Place ingredients in Dutch oven in the following order: meat, celery, onions, carrots and potatoes. Mix together, tomato juice, tapioca, sugar and salt, and pour over meat and vegetables. Tightly seal Dutch oven with aluminum foil and bake 4 hours at 250 degrees. Resist the temptation to peek, it will allow steam to escape. Sprinkle with parsley just before serving.
—Faye E. Moody

Alvah remembers this moose, a 1941 road kill, weighed in at 1600 pounds.

Kielbasa and Rice

2 cups cooked rice	1 cup sliced celery
1 tbsp. oleo	1 large cubed tomato
1 lb. sliced Kielbasa	1/2 tsp. garlic powder
1/2 cup chopped onion	1/2 tsp. thyme
1/2 cup diced green pepper	1/2 tsp. cayenne pepper
1 pkg. frozen peapods, optional	

Cook peapods and set aside. Melt oleo in 10-inch skillet and add kielbasa, onions, green pepper and celery. Saute until vegetables are tender. Add tomatoes and spices, and stir. Fold in rice and peapods. Heat through and serve.
—Alicia Mortensen

Judy's Beef Stroganof

1 lb. London broil	1 can (10-oz.)
1/2 cup chopped onion	cream of mushroom soup
1 can (4 oz.) mushrooms	1 cup sour cream
egg noodles	

Slice meat into long, thin strips. Saute chopped onion and sliced meat 5 minutes. Remove meat. Add mushroom soup, mushrooms and sour cream. Add meat, stir and cover. Reduce heat and simmer 30 minutes. Serve over cooked noodles.
—Debbie Moody Bellows

Steakburgers

1 egg	pepper
1/2 tsp. thyme	1/2 cup tomato paste
1/4 cup catsup	1 tbsp. mustard
1/2 cup chopped onion	1 cube beef bouillon
1 lb. ground beef	1 cup red wine
1/2 cup water	

Combine first 5 ingredients and pepper, and shape into patties; coat with flour and fry. Remove patties from skillet and set aside. Add remaining ingredients to skillet and simmer until thickened. Return patties to skillet, coat with sauce and serve.
—Naomi Walker

The Best Meatloaf

2 lbs. ground beef	1/2 cup catsup
2 eggs	1 1/2 tsp. salt
1/2 cup cracker crumbs	1/4 tsp. pepper
1/4 cup milk	1 pkg. onion soup mix

Combine all ingredients in large bowl and mix well. Shape meat in loaf pan and bake 60-75 minutes at 350 degrees.
—Laura Jones

Kaye's Meatloaf

1 1/2 lbs. ground beef	2 eggs
1 pkg. onion soup mix	1/2 cup milk
1 cup crushed cornflakes OR oatmeal	1/2 cup parmesan cheese
1/2 cup chopped green pepper, optional	

Combine all ingredients in large bowl and mix well. Shape meat in loaf pan and bake 60 minutes at 350 degrees.
---Rebecca Little

Meatloaf with Vegetables

1 lb. ground beef	salt and pepper to taste
2/3 cup milk	1 egg
1/3 cup breadcrumbs	2 tsp. Worcestershire sauce
1/4 cup catsup	
onions, carrots and potatoes enough for 4 people	

Beat egg and add milk. Add remaining ingredients and mix well. Place in casserole dish, cover and bake 1 hour at 350 degrees. Cook vegetables until nearly tender. Drain and place around meatloaf for last 30 minutes of baking. Uncover in last 10 minutes.
—Bertha Moody

Meatloaf Roll

1 lb. ground beef	1 tbsp. Italian seasoning
1/2 cup diced onion	1/4 tsp. pepper
2 eggs	1 tsp. salt
1 cup breadcrumbs	1 can (6 oz.) tomato sauce
1/4 cup diced green pepper	1 pkg.(8 oz.) mozarella cheese

Combine ground beef, eggs, breadcrumbs, onion and green pepper in large bowl. Mix well and add seasonings. Turn meat onto wax paper and flatten to 1/2-inch thick. Cover with sliced cheese and roll up meatloaf like jelly roll. Place in loaf pan and top with 2 slices cheese. Cover with tomato sauce and bake 1 hour at 350 degrees.
—Cathy Sprague

White Clam Sauce

1/4 cup olive oil	1/2 cup chopped parsley
1/4 cup oleo	1 tsp. oregano
3 minced garlic cloves	1 1/2-2 tbsp. flour
1/2 cup water	2 cans minced clams
2 tbsp. white wine, optional	
pepper to taste	

Heat oil and oleo in skillet; add garlic and cook until transluscent. Cool slightly and add water. Stir in parsley, pepper and oregano. Blend together flour and clam juice to make smooth paste and add to skillet. Stir well. Add clams and wine, and heat through. Serve over pasta with parmesan cheese.
—Dorothy Bruns Moody
Brian Moody contributed the same recipe but also adds 1 can (8 oz.) tomato sauce.

Capesante

A great scallop dish.

1/4 stick oleo	2/3 cup dry white wine
1 lb. bay scallops	1 tbsp. lemon juice
1 tbsp. ginger	1 cup whipping cream
1/2 lb. fresh mushrooms	3 tbsp. parmesan cheese
salt and freshly ground black pepper	

Melt oleo in large, flameproof skillet over medium-high heat. Add scallops, sliced mushrooms and ginger, and saute 2 minutes. Transfer scallops and mushrooms to platter and set aside. Add wine and lemon juice to skillet and cook until liquid is reduced by half. Blend in cream and continue cooking until again reduced by half. Return scallops and mushrooms to skillet, add salt and pepper, and heat through. Sprinkle with parmesan cheese and transfer to preheated broiler. Broil until slightly browned. Serve hot with rice.
—Nancy L. Moody

Baked Fish Fillets

1 lb. fish fillets	1/2 tsp. salt
2 tbsp. melted oleo	1/4 tsp. pepper
2 tbsp. lemon juice	2 cups Total cereal, crushed
1/4 tsp. dried dillweed, optional	

If fillets are large, cut into serving pieces. Combine oleo and lemon juice; set aside. Mix together salt, pepper and dillweed. Dip each fillet into melted oleo and sprinkle with spices. Coat with crushed cereal. Place fillets in greased, 9-inch pan and bake 25-30 minutes at 350 degrees, or until fish flakes easily with fork.
—Joan Moody

Baked Fish

2 lbs. haddock fillets	1 beaten egg
1/4 cup grated onion	1/2 cup cracker crumbs
2 tbsp. oleo	1 can (10 oz.) cream of shrimp soup

Place fillets in greased baking dish and dot with oleo. Combine remaining ingredients and pour over fish. Bake 1 hour at 400 degrees.
—Joan Moody

Mock Lobster Bake

1 lb. haddock fillets	1 tsp. prepared mustard
1/4 cup lemon juice	1/2 cup parmesan cheese
1/2 cup mayonnaise	paprika

Line 9 x 13 pan with foil. Place fillets in pan and sprinkle with lemon juice. Combine mayonnaise with mustard and spread over fish. Sprinkle generously with cheese and dash of paprika to simulate lobster. Bake 20 minutes at 400 degrees.
—Alicia Mortensen

Dottie's Salmon Loaf

2 cans (1 lb.) salmon, drained and flaked

1/2 cup fine breadcrumbs	1 tsp. parsley flakes
2 tbsp. melted oleo	1/2 tsp. salt
1 tsp. onion flakes	3 eggs, separated

dash of pepper
1 tbsp. chopped pimento, optional

Combine all ingredients except eggs in large bowl and toss lightly. Add beaten egg yolks and mix well. Beat egg whites until stiff and fold into batter. Pour into greased loaf pan and bake 45 minutes at 350 degrees. Serve hot with lemon or white sauce, or cold with tart mayonnaise.
—Debbie Moody Bellows

Lupiers

A Philippino treat.

2 pkgs. eggroll wrappers	1 crushed garlic clove
2 lbs. ground beef	2 tbsp. oleo
1/2 cup chopped onion	pepper to taste
1/2 cup chopped green pepper	1 small jar jalapeno relish

1 cup grated Cheddar cheese

Saute onions, green peppers and garlic in oleo. Add ground beef and brown. Drain meat; add jalapeno relish and pepper, and simmer 10 minutes. Fill eggroll wrappers each with 2-3 tbsp. meat and 2 tbsp. cheese, roll up and deep fry until browned.
—Charlene Ward

Subgum

1 can (4 oz.) sliced mushrooms	2 cups chopped Chinese cabbage
1 1/2 cups cubed, cooked pork	1 1/2 cups prepared pork gravy
2 cups sliced celery	1 can (14 oz.) bean sprouts
1 tbsp. oleo	2 tsp. soy sauce
1 cup sliced green pepper	1 tbsp. honey
1 can (4 oz.) drained water chestnuts	2-3 cups chow mein noodles OR rice
1 pkg. frozen peapods	

Cook together mushrooms, pork, celery, green pepper, cabbage and chestnuts in oleo until tender — approximately 10 minutes. Add gravy and stir until thickened. Add honey and stir. Reduce heat and simmer 15 minutes. Add soy sauce, bean sprouts and peapods. Heat through and serve over chow mein noodle or rice. Chicken, scallops or beef can be substituted for pork.
—Alicia Mortensen

Enchiladas Supreme

2 cups cooked beef OR chicken	1 can (8 oz.) enchilada sauce
1 cup sour cream	8 soft, corn tortillas
1/2 can (4 oz.) diced green chilis	1 can (8 oz.) tomato sauce
1/4 cup sliced black olives	2 tbsp. olive oil
2 chopped green onions	1 cup grated Cheddar cheese

Heat oil until hot and dip one side of tortillas in oil for 5 seconds. Stack and drain on napkins. In large skillet, combine and heat sauces. Cover bottom of large baking dish with 1/4 of sauce. Combine meat, chilis and olives in sour cream. Scoop 2 tbsp. meat into each tortilla, fold sides over meat and place in baking dish. Pour sauce over enchiladas and sprinkle with cheese. Top with chopped green onion and bake 35-40 minutes at 350, until cheese melts.
—Clara Moody Kiener

Fajitas

1 lb. cooked, boned and skinned chicken	
5 tbsp. oil	1/2 tsp. pepper
2 tbsp. lemon juice	1 cup sliced green pepper
1 tsp. garlic powder	1 cup sliced onion wedges
1 tsp. seasoned salt	1 cup sliced tomato wedges
1/2 tsp. oregano	1/2 cup chunky taco salsa
8 hot corn OR flour tortillas	

In medium bowl, combine meat, 2 tbsp. oil, juice and spices. Cover and marinate in refrigerator 6-9 hours. In 10-inch cast iron skillet, heat 3 tbsp. oil until very hot. Saute half the meat until just browned; add half the peppers and onions, and cook 1-2 minutes. Remove from skillet. Add remaining meat and cook, then add remaining peppers and onions, and cook until crisp-tender. Return all meat and vegetables to skillet, add tomato and salsa. Simmer 1 minute, tossing to coat with salsa.
—Lynne Weister

——— Casseroles ———

Beef and Corn Casserole

1 tbsp. oil	1/2 cup grated sharp cheese
1/4 lb. dried beef	2 cups whole kernel corn, drained
1 cup sliced mushrooms	2 cups medium white sauce
1/4 cup chopped onion	2 egg yolks, beaten
1/4 cup chopped green pepper	1 tsp. prepared mustard
1/4 tsp. paprika	

Cook onion and green pepper in oil until tender. Add beef and mushrooms, and cook until dried beef frizzles at edges. Blend together white sauce, egg yolks and mustard. (Use white sauce recipe from Fish Casserole.) Combine with beef mixture, add corn and pour mixture into 1 1/2 quart casserole dish. Sprinkle with grated cheese and paprika. Bake 30 minutes at 350 degrees.
—Rayetta Flint

Baked Rice Casserole

1 can (10 oz.) onion soup	1/2 stick oleo
1 can (10 oz.) beef consomme	1 can (4 oz.) can sliced mushrooms
1 1/4 cups long grain rice	

Place all ingredients in casserole dish; cover with foil. Bake 30 minutes at 350 degrees. Remove foil, stir and bake uncovered 30 minutes longer.
—Judy Moody Beck

Rice Casserole

1 cup long grain rice	1/2 stick oleo
2 cans (10 oz.) beef bouillon	1 onion, finely chopped

Combine all ingredients in casserole dish and stir. Bake uncovered 1 hour at 350 degrees.
—Bev Eaton

Clam Casserole

4 tbsp. oleo	2 cups crushed saltine crackers
2 cans minced clams, not drained	2 beaten eggs
1 tbsp. dill weed	2 cups milk
	dash of pepper

Melt oleo and coat casserole dish. Combine clams and juice, dill weed, saltines and eggs. Add milk, pepper and pour into casserole. Sprinkle with paprika. Let stand 2 hours, then bake 30 minutes at 350 degrees.
—Deborah M. Pooley

Carefree Casserole

1/2 cups instant rice	1/4 cup chopped onion
1 tbsp. oleo	1 cup cooked peas
1 1/4 cups water	1/2 tsp. each salt and pepper
1 can (10 oz.) cream of mushroom soup	1/2 cup grated Cheddar cheese
2 cups diced, cooked chicken OR drained, flaked tuna	

Measure rice into 1 1/2 quart casserole. In separate pan, saute onion in oleo until translucent; blend in mushroom soup and water. Stir in chicken or tuna, cooked peas, salt and pepper. Bring to boil, stirring occasionally. Stir mixture into rice and sprinkle with grated cheese. Cover and bake 20 minutes at 400 degrees. Stir before serving.
—Corrine Perkins

Chicken or Turkey Bake

3 cups cooked chicken OR turkey	1 can (6 oz.) sliced water chestnuts
2 cups diced celery	1/2 cup sliced almonds
2 cups cooked long grain rice	1 cup mayonnaise
2 cans (10 oz.) cream of chicken soup	cornflakes to cover
4 tbsp. chopped onion	1/4 cup melted oleo

Mix all ingredients except cornflakes and oleo, and pour into casserole dish. Top with cornflakes and melted oleo. Bake 35-40 minutes at 350 degrees. This casserole can be made a day ahead and stored in the refrigerator. Top with cornflakes before cooking.
—Jan Jones

Chicken and Rice Casserole

1 cup long grain rice	1 can (10 oz.) cream of mushroom soup
1 pkg. onion soup mix	2 cups water
4-5 chicken breasts	

Combine first four ingredients in greased casserole dish. Top with chicken breasts, cover and bake at 350 degrees until done — about 1 hr.
—Pat Caldwell

Hearty Casserole

1 lb. ground beef	4-5 celery stalks, cut in 1/2 inch pieces
2 med. onions, thinly sliced	3-4 medium potatoes, quartered
3-4 carrots, cut in 1 inch pieces	2 tbsp. oleo
1/4 tsp. pepper	1/2 tsp. salt
3 tbsp. flour	

Shape ground beef into patties and brown in oleo. Arrange browned patties in bottom of greased casserole. Arrange vegetables in layers over meat. Add flour to pan drippings; add salt and pepper. Add 1 1/2-2 cups water to make medium gravy; pour over vegetables. Cover and bake 1 1/4 hours at 375 degrees.
—Charlene Ward

Hungry Boys Casserole

1 lb. lean ground beef	1 lb. can baked beans
1/2 cup chopped celery	1/4 cup catsup
1/4 cup chopped onion	1/4 cup water
1/4 cup chopped green pepper	1/2 tsp. salt
1/2 tsp. garlic salt	

Sprinkle celery, onion and green pepper in bottom of casserole dish. Crumble ground beef on top and bake 20 minutes, uncovered, at 425 degrees. Remove from oven; stir in water, baked beans, catsup, water, salt and garlic salt. Return casserole to oven for 20-30 minutes longer.
—Judy Moody Beck

Mom's Macaroni and Cheese

2 cups elbow macaroni, cooked and drained

2 tbsp. oleo	dash pepper
1/2 tsp. salt	2 cups milk
3 tbsp. flour	2 cups shredded Cheddar cheese

Melt oleo over low heat and add flour, salt, pepper. Add milk; and stir until thickened. Add cheese. When cheese is melted, add to macaroni in 1 1/2 quart casserole. Bake 30 minutes at 350 degrees.
—Rachel Little

Macaroni and Cheese

1 cup elbow macaroni, cooked and drained	1/2 lb. shredded Cheddar cheese
2 tbsp. flour	2 tbsp. oleo
1/2 tsp. salt	1 cup milk

Melt oleo in double boiler. Add flour, salt and pepper; blend well. Add milk slowly, stirring constantly, and cook until sauce thickens. Add cheese and stir until melted. Pour sauce over noodles. Bake 30 minutes at 350 degrees.
—Chris Reed

Italian Macaroni and Beef

1 lb. ground beef	1/2 cup drained tomatoes
1/4 cup finely chopped green pepper	2 tbsp. oleo
3/4 cup chopped onion	3 tbsp. flour
1 tsp. basil	2 cups milk
1 tsp. oregano	10 oz. grated Cheddar cheese
salt and pepper to taste	
parmesan cheese	
1 1/2 cups cooked, drained elbow macaroni	

Brown meat, onions and pepper. Add basil, oregano and tomatoes; cook 3 minutes. In separate pan, make white sauce with oleo, flour and milk. Add cheese and cook until thickened. Add salt and pepper. Combine meat, macaroni and 2/3 of sauce in 9 x 13 pan. Cover with remaining sauce and sprinkle with parmesan. Cover and bake 20-25 minutes at 450 degrees. Remove cover and cook 2-3 minutes longer.
—Jan Jones

Spaghetti Casserole

2 tbsp. oleo	2 cups stewed tomatoes
1/2 cup chopped onion	1 1/2 cups uncooked spaghetti
1 lb. ground beef	1/2 cup catsup
3/4 cup water	pinch oregano
salt and pepper to taste	

Saute onion in oleo; add ground beef, salt and oregano. Break spaghetti in pieces and place half in casserole dish. Cover with half the cooked ground beef and 1 cup tomatoes. Repeat layers. Mix water and catsup, and pour over layers. Cover. Bake 45 minutes at 350 degrees OR microwave 22 minutes on High.
—Doris Moody Eaton

Spaghetti Pie

8 oz. spaghetti, cooked and drained	dash oregano
1 egg	2 cups spaghetti sauce
2 tbsp. oil	8 oz. mozarella cheese
pepperoni, ham or ground beef, optional	

Mix spaghetti with egg, oil and oregano. Spread in 9-inch pie plate to form "crust." Fill with meat sauce and top with cheese. Bake 30 minutes at 350 degrees. Cut in slices to serve.
—Mary Olson

Bill Sackett

His first trip to Moody's was a memorable one for photographer Bill Sackett, as his letter explains:

"My first stop at Moody's Diner may have saved my life!! I had bought a motorcycle that summer, and was riding from Vermont up the Maine coast. It was quite cold, and very late, and very foggy that evening. I was chilled to the bone, and getting a bit shakey... not the ideal set of reflexes for riding an unfamilar motorcycle. Out of the fog popped Moody's Diner! I stopped for coffee, bringing it out to the curb, where I sat sipping from a styrofoam cup. It happened I'd parked beside a pickup truck with a motorcycle loaded in the back. When the driver returned, he struck up a conversation. This man told me I should be careful of a bridge up the road, since it had an odd, metal grate surface, and it had a way of throwing bikes out of control. 'Just lighten up your grip, and give it its head, and you'll go right through with no problem,' he told me. 'But if you bear down on 'er, she'll buckle.'

"When I hit that bridge later, I did as he'd said, and went right through. Without that advice, though, my reflexes would have been wrong!

"And by the way, someone did me a great favor later on, and stole the silly motorcycle."

Spaghetti Pie II

6 oz. spaghetti, cooked and drained	1/4 cup chopped green pepper
2 tbsp. oleo	1 cup stewed tomatoes
2 well-beaten eggs	1 can (6 oz.) tomato paste
1/3 cup grated parmesan cheese	1 tsp. sugar
1 cup cottage cheese	1 tsp. oregano
1 lb. ground beef	1/2 tsp. garlic salt
1/2 cup chopped onion	1/2 cup shredded mozarella

Stir oleo into hot spaghetti. Stir in parmesan cheese and eggs. Spread spaghetti and egg mixture into 10-inch pie plate, forming "crust." Spread cottage cheese over spaghetti crust. In skillet, cook together beef, onion and green pepper. Drain off excess fat. Stir in tomatoes, tomato paste, sugar, oregano and garlic salt. Heat through. Spread meat and tomato sauce over cottage cheese. and bake 20 minutes at 350 degrees. Sprinkle with mozarella. Return to oven and bake until cheese melts.
—Linda Moody Davis

Easy Ziti Casserole

1/2 box ziti, cooked and drained	4 cups spaghetti sauce
1/4 cup chopped onion	8 oz. shredded mozarella cheese
1 lb. ground beef	sliced pepperoni

Pour cooked ziti into 9 x 13 pan. Brown beef and onion, and pour over ziti. Top with spaghetti sauce, cheese and pepperoni. Bake 30 minutes at 350 degrees.
—Anne Braley

Italian Zucchini Casserole

2-2 1/2 lbs. zucchini	1 can (6 oz.) tomato paste
4 tbsp. oleo	1 cup water
1/2 cup chopped onion	1/2 cup shredded Cheddar cheese
1/2 cup chopped green pepper	1 pkg. spaghetti sauce mix
1 can (4 oz.) mushrooms	grated parmesan cheese

Slice zucchini into 1/2 inch pieces and drop into boiling water. Cook 4-5 minutes and drain. Place zucchini in casserole dish. Saute onion and green pepper in oleo. Add sauce mix, cheese, mushrooms, tomato paste and water. Mix well and pour over zucchini. Sprinkle top with parmesan cheese. Bake 25-30 minutes at 350 degrees, or microwave 13 minutes on High; turn once. Let stand 5-10 minutes before serving.
—Carol Hallowell

Zucchini Casserole

2-3 medium zucchini, thinly sliced   2-3 chopped tomatoes
2 onions, thinly sliced   1 cup shredded sharp Cheddar cheese
2 tbsp. oil

Saute onions, zucchini and tomatoes in oil. Cook over low heat until tender, stirring occasionally. Pour into casserole dish and sprinkle with shredded cheese. Bake 30 minutes at 350 degrees.
—Nellie Jones

Quickie Casserole

2 cups cooked shrimp   1/2 cup milk
2 cups cooked macaroni   1 cup cooked peas
1/4 cup diced onions   salt and pepper to taste
1/4 cup parmesan cheese   2 cups crushed saltines
1 can (10 oz.) cream of chicken soup   1/4 cup melted oleo

Mix all ingredients, except crackers and oleo, in 3 quart casserole dish. Mix saltines with melted oleo and sprinkle on top. Bake 30 minutes at 350 degrees. Cooked chicken or canned tuna can be used instead of shrimp.
—Alicia Mortensen

Fish Casserole

1 lb. potatoes, thinly sliced   3 tbsp. flour
1 lb. firm white fish, cooked and flaked   2 tbsp. oleo
1/2 cup chopped onion   2 cups milk
salt and pepper to taste

In a buttered casserole dish, layer potatoes, fish and onion; season with salt and pepper. Cheese, peas, mushrooms or boiled eggs can be added to the layers.
Make white sauce with flour, oleo and milk. Pour sauce over layers in casserole. Bake 1 hour at 350 degrees or until potates are soft.
—Debbie Moody Bellows

Scallop Casserole

2 lbs. scallops, quartered and sauteed 1/8 tsp. pepper
1 box (12 oz.) cooked, drained noodles 4 cups milk
6 tbsp. oleo 2 cans (4 oz.) mushrooms, drained
6 tbsp. flour 1/2 cup cooking sherry
1/2 tsp. salt 1/2 lb. grated sharp Cheddar cheese

Pour noodles into greased 4 quart casserole dish. In separate pan, melt oleo; blend in flour, salt and pepper. Cook over low heat until smooth. Slowly add milk and cook until sauce thickens, stirring constantly. Add scallops, mushrooms and sherry to sauce. Pour over noodles, lifting with fork to blend. Top with grated cheese. Cover and bake 45-50 minutes at 350 degrees.
—Sharon Moody

Tuna Wiggle

1 can (10 oz.) cream of mushroom soup 1 can (6 oz.) tuna, drained and flaked
1/2 cup cooked peas 1 tsp. Worcestershire sauce

Combine all ingredients in top of double boiler and heat through. Serve over saltine crackers. For unexpected guests, add 1 can evaporated milk and thicken with flour.
—Bertha Moody

Tuna Mushroom Casserole

1 cup uncooked long grain rice 1 pkg. (10 oz.) frozen peas
1 can (10 oz.) cream of mushroom soup 1 can (6 oz.) tuna, drained and flaked
2 1/4 cups water 1 tbsp. Worcestershire sauce
1/2 cup chopped onion 1 can (4 oz.) mushroom pieces, drained

Combine rice, soup, water, onion and Worcestershire sauce in large skillet. Stir well and bring to boil. Reduce heat, cover and cook over low heat about 25 minutes. OR until rice is tender. Stir occasionally. Fold in peas, tuna and mushroom pieces. Heat uncovered 5 minutes.
—Peggy Jones

Dynamites

6 celery stalks, chopped	salt and pepper to taste
4 chopped onions	2 quarts spaghetti sauce
5 chopped green peppers	1 can (6 oz.) tomato paste
pinch oregano	1 can (16 oz.) tomatoes
pinch garlic salt	2 drops Tabasco sauce
2 1/2 lbs. ground beef, browned	

Cook celery, onions, green peppers, oregano and garlic until tender. Add spaghetti sauce, tomato paste, tomatoes, Tabasco and ground beef. Heat through. Serve on toasted hot dog rolls with hot, crushed peppers and shredded cheese.
—Frances Creamer

Tuna Warm-Ups

1 can (6 oz.) tuna, drained and flaked	1 tbsp. chopped sweet pickle
3 chopped hard-boiled eggs	1/2 cup grated cheese
1 tbsp. chopped onion	1/2 cup mayonnaise
hot dog rolls	

Mix together all ingredients. Butter 12 hot dog rolls and fill with tuna mixture. Toast in frying pan OR wrap in foil and bake 15 minutes at 400 degrees.
—Frances Creamer

This is one of the few photographs we were able to find that was taken inside the diner. Most people used simple box cameras, like the Brownie, and didn't have flash attachments. If you wanted to take a picture you went outside. Sitting behind the counter is Arlene Aho.

—— Vegetables ——

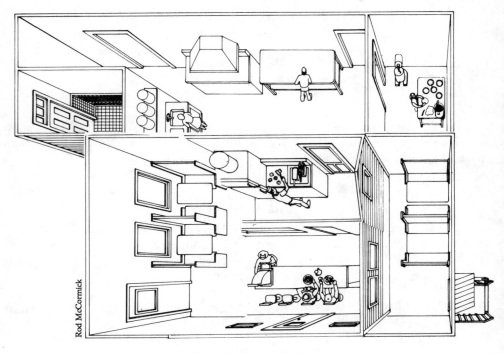

Moody's Diner 1940

Broccoli Casserole

1 medium onion, chopped	1/4 cup water
1/2 stick oleo	1/2 cup cheese whiz
1 can cream of chicken soup	1 pkg. (8 oz.) cooked broccoli
1/2 cup milk	1 cup minute rice

Saute onion in oleo until transparent. Add soup, water, milk and cheese whiz. Stir until smooth. Grease casserole dish, put rice and drained broccoli on bottom. Pour sauce over rice and broccoli and bake 40-50 minutes at 350 degrees.
—Dot Aho Moody

Creamed Cabbage

1 small cabbage	3 tbsp. butter
2 tsp. oil	1/2 cup cream

Cut cabbage into bite-size pieces. Bring pot of salted water to boil. Add oil to boiling water, then cook cabbage in water until tender. Drain, and add butter and cream.
—Marge Adams

Sweet and Sour Red Cabbage

1 red cabbage	1 stick oleo
1 cup water	3 tbsp. salt
1 cup cider vinegar	1 1/2 cups sugar
1 cup applesauce	

Shred cabbage and place in saucepan. Add water, vinegar, oleo, salt and sugar. Bring to a boil, then stir in applesauce. Simmer one hour.
—Carolyn Staples

Marinated Carrots

1 lb. carrots	2 medium onions
1 large green pepper	10 oz. French dressing

Peel and slice carrots into saucepan and boil until just tender. Drain and pour into a bowl. Chop peppers and onions and add to carrots. Mix in French dressing and refrigerate a few hours or overnight.
—Judy Moody Beck

Corn Souffle

1 tbsp. butter	1/4 tsp. salt
2 tbsp. flour	1/4 tsp. pepper
1 cup milk	1 can (16 oz.) creamed corn
2 eggs, separated	

Melt butter, add flour and milk and bring to a boil. Remove from heat and add salt and pepper. Stir in creamed corn and beaten egg yolks. Beat egg whites until stiff and fold into batter. Pour into buttered baking dish. Bake 35-40 minutes at 350 degrees.
—Alice Wellman

Company Green Beans

1/2 lb. fresh mushrooms	lemon pepper
2 tbsp. butter	3 tbsp. white wine
garlic salt	1 can (16 oz.) green beans
sliced toasted almonds	

Slice and saute mushrooms in butter until tender. Season with salt and lemon pepper, add wine and simmer. Drain and rinse green beans twice in cold water, then add to mushrooms and cook about 45 minutes until liquid is almost gone. Sprinkle sliced almonds over beans and serve.
—Clara Moody Kiener

Pea Salad

1 small chopped onion
2 chopped hard-boiled eggs
4 oz. cubed Cheddar cheese
sweet pickle relish
salt and pepper to taste
mayonnaise
2 cans peas OR
1 package (1 lb.) cooked frozen peas

Combine all ingredients, adding just enough mayonnaise to moisten salad Chill before serving.
—Charlene Moody Ward

Potato Pie

1 lb. potatoes   2 tbsp. oleo
1 med. yellow onion   nutmeg
2 tbsp. oil   salt andpepper
1 chopped clove garlic
1 cup grated cheese (Cheddar or guyere)

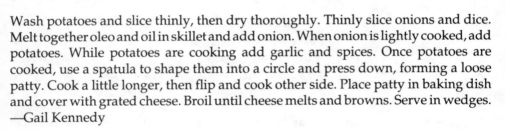

Wash potatoes and slice thinly, then dry thoroughly. Thinly slice onions and dice. Melt together oleo and oil in skillet and add onion. When onion is lightly cooked, add potatoes. While potatoes are cooking add garlic and spices. Once potatoes are cooked, use a spatula to shape them into a circle and press down, forming a loose patty. Cook a little longer, then flip and cook other side. Place patty in baking dish and cover with grated cheese. Broil until cheese melts and browns. Serve in wedges.
—Gail Kennedy

Scalloped Onions with Cheese Sauce

4-6 medium onions   2 cups milk
1/4 cup oleo   1/2 tsp. salt
1/4 cup flour   2 cups sharp Cheddar cheese

Thinly slice onions and place into 1 1/2 quart casserole dish. Melt oleo in skillet and blend in flour. Add milk and cook over low heat until thickened, stirring constantly. Add salt and grated cheese, stir until cheese melts. Pour sauce over onions and bake 1 hour at 350 degrees.
—Faye E. Moody

Spinach Casserole

1 pkg. chopped spinach, cooked	1 can (10 oz.) mushroom soup
1 tbsp. grated onion	1 cup stuffing mix
3/4 cup grated sharp cheese	1/4 cup oleo
1 beaten egg	

Combine all ingredients and mix well. Pour in greased casserole dish and bake 30 minutes at 350 degrees.
—Thelma Moody

Rose's Baked Beans

2 cups beans (yellow-eyed or pea beans)
1/2 cup brown sugar 1 tsp. prepared mustard
1/2 tsp. salt 1/2 tsp. ginger
dash of pepper dash of paprika
2 tbsp. shortening

Cover beans with cold water and soak overnight. Drain beans and place in bean pot. Mix brown sugar, salt, pepper, mustard, ginger and paprika with a little hot water and pour over beans. Add shortening and cover beans with hot water. Cover pot and bake 6 hours at 325 degrees. Check often, adding hot water as needed. Cover may be removed for last hour.
—Nancy Moody Genthner

Dewey and Nellie taking a break outside Moody's Diner.

Nellie: *One time a prisoner escaped from Thomaston and Dewey was sure he saw him up in the tree. He sat on the bank and watched him down at the diner. There were police and guards all over looking for him.*

Alvah: *Dewey kept saying, "That's him in the tree." No one would listen to him. They caught him the next day. Sure enough it was him up in that tree.*

—— Desserts ——

Bread Pudding

4 slices bread, cubed   3/4 cup sugar
3 cups milk   1/4 tsp. salt
1 beaten egg   1/2 tsp. nutmeg
1/2 cup seedless raisins

In saucepan, heat bread in half of the milk. When hot, add remaining milk, then add other ingredients. Pour into casserole dish and bake 1 hour at 350 degrees. Stir occasionally.
—Jean Moody

Gingerbread

1 egg   1 cup flour
1/2 cup sugar   1 tsp. baking soda
1/4 cup molasses   1/2 tsp. salt
1/4 cup melted shortening   1 tsp. ginger
1/2 cup boiling water

Mix together egg and sugar, then add molasses and shortening. Mix well. Stir in dry ingredients and then the hot water. Pour batter into greased and floured 8-inch pan. Bake 30 minutes at 350 degrees. Serve hot with whipped cream.
—Bertha Moody

Gingerbread II

1/2 cup shortening   1 1/2 tsp. baking soda
1/2 cup sugar   1 tsp. cinnamon
1 egg   3/4 tsp. ginger
1 cup molasses   1/2 tsp. cloves
2 1/2 cups flour   1/2 tsp. salt
1 cup hot water

Mix shortening, sugar, egg and molasses and beat well. Sift together dry ingredients and add to egg batter. Stir in hot water. Pour into 8-inch pan and bake 45-50 minutes at 350 degrees.
—Sharon Moody

Indian Pudding

5 tbsp. cornmeal	1 tsp. salt
1 quart milk	3/4 tsp. cinnamon
2 tbsp. oleo	1/2 tsp. ginger
3/4 cup molasses	2 well beaten eggs
1 cup evaporated milk	

Scald the milk with the cornmeal added, then mix in oleo, molasses, salt, spices and eggs. Pour into a well-greased dish, add the evaporated milk but do not stir. Bake 1 hour at 350 degrees. Serve warm with a scoop of ice cream.
—Cynthia Hilton

Blueberry Crisp

1 cup oatmeal	1/2 tsp. salt
1/3 cup flour	1 tsp. cinnamon
1/2 cup brown sugar	1/3 cup softened oleo
2 cups blueberries	

Pour blueberries into 8-inch casserole dish. In a separate bowl, combine and mix other ingredients until crumbly, then sprinkle over blueberries. Bake 35-40 minutes at 350 degrees. Serve warm topped with whipped cream or ice cream.
—Andrea Moody Newbert

Cherry Blossom Dessert

Filling:

1/4 cup flour	1 cup sugar
1/4 tsp. almond extract	1/4 tsp. red food coloring
3/4 cup cherry juice from 1 can cherries	

Combine ingredients in saucepan and cook over medium heat until thickened. Add cherries.

1 1/2 cups flour	1 cup packed brown sugar
1 tsp. salt	1 cup quick-cooking oatmeal
1/2 tsp. baking soda	1/2 cup shortening

Sift flour, salt and baking soda. Blend in brown sugar and oatmeal and cut in shortening. Press half the oatmeal batter into ungreased 8-inch pan. Spread with cooled cherry filling and cover with the remaining oatmeal batter. Bake 25-30 minutes at 350 degrees. Serve with whipped cream or ice cream.
—Nancy Moody Genthner

Grapefruit Baked Alaska

3 egg whites	2 grapefruit
1/4 tsp. cream of tartar	vanilla ice cream
6 tbsp. sugar	

Beat egg whites with cream of tartar until soft peaks form.Gradually beat in sugar until egg whites are stiff and glossy. Cut grapefruit in half and section them. Place scoop of ice cream on each grapefruit and carefully cover with meringue. (See Pies for meringue recipe.) Brown quickly in 450 degree oven. Serve immediately.
—Brian Moody

Strawberry Rhubarb Puff

1 quart (3 cups) chopped rhubarb	3 tsp. baking powder
1 quart sliced strawberries	1 tsp. salt
1 1/2 cups sugar OR	1/3 cup oil
3/4 cup honey	2/3 cup milk
2 cups flour	2 tbsp. sugar
2 tbsp. sugar	1 tsp. cinnamon
	butter

Mix together rhubarb, strawberries and 1 1/2 cups sugar, and place in ungreased 9-inch baking pan. Place in 350 degree oven. Mix flour, 2 tbsp. sugar, baking powder and salt in bowl. Pour oil and milk into measuring cup -- don't mix -- and stir into flour. Stir until dough cleans sides of bowl and forms into a ball. Drop dough by spoonfuls onto hot fruit. Make an indentation in each drop of dough and dot with butter. Mix remaining sugar with cinnamon and sprinkle over dough. Return to oven and bake 20-25 minutes. Serve warm.
—Debbie Moody Bellows

Rhubarb Dessert

1 cup flour	1 1/2 cups sugar
5 tbsp. powdered sugar	1/4 cup flour
1/2 cup oleo	3/4 tsp. baking powder
2 eggs	1 tsp. vanilla
2 cups chopped rhubarb	

Mix 1 cup flour, powdered sugar and oleo together to consistency of pie crust dough. Pat into 9-inch baking pan. Bake 15 minutes at 350 degrees until crust is golden brown. Beat eggs, add sugar and mix thoroughly, then add remaining ingredients. Pour over crust and bake 30 minutes at 350 degrees.
—Jean Moody

Eggless Chocolate Pudding

2/3 cup sugar   3 tbsp. cocoa
1/4 cup cornstarch   2 3/4 cups milk
1/8 tsp. salt   2 tbsp. oleo
1 tsp. vanilla

Mix together sugar, cornstarch, salt and cocoa. Gradually add milk and pour into saucepan. Bring to boil over medium heat, stirring constantly. Boil 1 minute and remove from heat. Stir in oleo and vanilla. Chill and serve. For eggless vanilla pudding, omit 1/3 cup sugar and cocoa.
—Alice Wellman

Mom's Chocolate Pudding

1 can (12-oz.) evaporated milk   2 rounded tbsp. cornstarch
1 1/2 cups water   4 level tbsp. cocoa
1 cup sugar   1/2 tsp. salt
1 tsp. vanilla

Heat evaporated milk and water in double boiler. Mix together sugar, cornstarch, cocoa and salt. Add 3-5 tbsp. hot milk to the dry ingredients and stir until smooth. Add cocoa mixture to heated milk and cook, stirring until thickened. Cool, and add vanilla. Serve with whipped cream.
—Judy Moody Beck

Chocolate Torte

1 stick oleo   1 cup powdered sugar
1 cup flour   12 oz. cool whip
1/2 cup chopped nuts   2 pkgs. (3 oz.) instant chocolate pudding
8 oz. cream cheese   3 cups cold milk

Mix oleo, flour and nuts and pat into 13 x 9 pan. Bake 15 minutes at 350 degrees and cool. Beat together cream cheese and sugar. Add 1/2 of cool whip and spread over crust. Beat pudding with milk and spread over cream cheese. Top with remaining cool whip and decorate with chopped nuts. Refrigerate until served.
—Jan Jones

Refrigerator Pie

1 1/2 cups flour   1 cup powdered sugar
3/4 cup oleo   2 cups cool whip
3/4 cup chopped pecans OR walnuts   2 pkgs. (3 oz.) instant lemon pudding
8 oz. cream cheese   3 cups milk

Blend flour, oleo and chopped nuts. Press into a 13 x 9 pan. Bake 10-15 minutes at 350 degrees and let cool. Beat cream cheese and powdered sugar, and blend in 1 cup cool whip. Spread over cooled crust. Combine pudding and milk, and mix until thickened. Spread over cream cheese, and spread with remaining cool whip. Refrigerate.
—Jean Moody

Gillie Whoopers

1/2 cup oleo	1/4 tsp. salt
3/4 cup sugar	2 tbsp. cocoa
2 eggs	1 tsp. vanilla
3/4 cup sifted flour	1/2 cup chopped nuts
1/4 tsp. baking powder	1 pkg. miniature marshmallows

Cream oleo, then add sugar. Add eggs one at a time, beating after each addition. Add sifted dry ingredients and stir well. Add vanilla and chopped nuts. Pour batter into greased 9-inch pan and bake 25 minutes at 350 degrees. Remove from oven and sprinkle marshmallows on top, keeping away from edges. Return to oven for 2 minutes. Remove from oven and frost.

Frosting:

1/2 cup light brown sugar	3 tsp. oleo
1/4 cup water	1 tsp. vanilla
2 squares unsweetened chocolate	1 1/2 cups powdered sugar

Combine brown sugar, water and chocolate and boil three minutes. Add remaining ingredients, mix and spread over marshmallows. Cool and cut in squares.
—Naomi Walker

Marian Savage

Some of the photographs in this book were taken by Marian Savage during the summer of 1975. Marian had come to Maine to take a course at the Maine Photographic Workshop in Rockport. After hunting up her negatives for inclusion in this collection, Marian remembered her time spent with P.B. Moody and family:

Before coming to Maine I had waitressed tables at a seafood restaurant in Maryland. That restaurant specialized in Maryland hard-shell crab, yet most of what was served was shipped in from Texas and Louisiana. Most of our "fresh seafood" was frozen, shipped in from other places. The soups were canned, the desserts processed, and the dinnerware was made of styrofoam. So you can imagine how refreshing it was to find Moody's Diner. Home made desserts, fresh seafood, real mashed potatoes, I was immediately taken in.

Later, when I'd come up with the idea of doing a photographic study of P.B. Moody, he seemed both flattered and puzzled. But when I tagged along during the next four days he seemed totalled unaffected by the presence of my camera and me.

Following P.B. Moody around was no easy task however. He was 75 at the time. Although he had a crew with him no one worked harder during haying than P.B. Up at the house while I was chatting with Bertha Moody he went off to tinker with his car, or into the barn to move hay bales preparing for the new load to come in, or he'd be off to pick strawberries, or on his hands and knees scrubbing the kitchen floor in the diner. He was always busy with something.

He once told me that he was an enterprising person, that he looked to deliver a product at a good value to customers and charge enough to make a profit. He started out by selling hot dogs at baseball games, and cutting and selling Christmas trees.

I was invited to attend a family reunion at Moody's Island. I had a wonderful time, a friendlier family doesn't exist. That was my last full day with the Moody's. Later that winter I moved to Maine for good.

It is interesting to note that Patrick Downs, who also contributed fine photographs to this book, came to Maine to study photography at the Maine Photographic Workshop in Rockport. Downs is a photographer with the *L.A. Times*, Savage is Circulation Director for *National Fisherman* and *Seafood Business* magazines.

Millionaire's Pie

1 pkg. Lorna Doone cookies   2 slightly beaten eggs
3/4 cup softened oleo   1 cup whipped cream OR
1 1/2 cup cup powdered sugar   small container cool whip
1 can (20-oz.) crushed pineapple, well drained

Crush cookies and set aside 1/4 cup. Mix remaining cookies with 1/4 cup oleo and press into ungreased 9 x 13 pan. Bake 15 minutes at 300 degrees. Remove from oven and cool. Cream remaining oleo with sugar, mix in eggs and spread over cookie crust. Combine pineapple and whipped cream and spread over above layer. Sprinkle top with 1/4 cup reserved cookie crumbs. Refrigerate topped with foil, and store for a day if possible. Cut into squares and serve.
—Pat Caldwell

Cheese Cake

3 pkgs. (8 oz.) softened cream cheese   1 package (3-oz.) instant vanilla pudding
2 tsp. vanilla   4 egg whites, stiffly beaten
1 cup sugar   1 stick oleo
4 egg yolks   1/4 cup sugar
1 1/2 pints sour cream   1 1/4 cups graham cracker crumbs

Beat cream cheese, vanilla, sugar and egg yolks until creamy and free of lumps. Add sour cream and pudding, and mix again. Fold in beaten egg whites and set aside. Mix oleo with graham cracker crumbs and sugar and press into 9-inch springform pan. Pour in cream cheese filling and bake 1 hour at 350 degrees. Don't open the oven door while baking. Turn off oven, leave cake in 1 hour to prevent cake from cracking.
—Irene Duprey

Pumpkin Cake Roll

3 eggs   1 tsp. ginger
1 cup sugar   1/2 tsp. salt
2/3 cup pumpkin   1 cup powdered sugar
1 tsp. lemon juice   2 pkgs. (3 oz.) cream cheese
3/4 cup flour   4 tbsp. oleo
1 tsp. baking powder   1/2 tsp. vanilla
2 tsp. cinnamon   1 /2 cup chopped nuts

Beat eggs with electric mixer on high for 5 minutes. Gradually add sugar, stir in pumpkin and add lemon juice. In a separate bowl, stir together flour, baking powder, cinnamon, ginger and salt. Fold dry ingredients into pumpkin and spread into greased and floured 15 x 10 pan. Bake 15 minutes at 375 degrees. Turn cake onto a towel sprinkled with powdered sugar. Roll cake and towel together and let cool. Beat together powdered sugar, cream cheese, oleo and vanilla. Beat until smooth. Carefully unroll cake and spread with cream cheese and nuts. Roll and chill. Sprinkle with powdered sugar and serve.
—Anne Braley

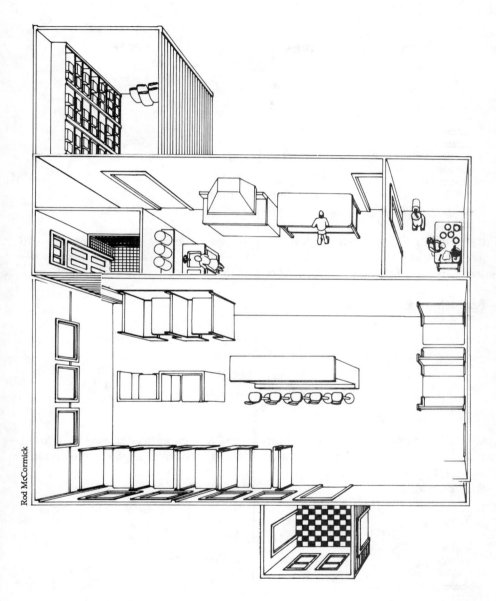

Rod McCormick

Moody's Diner 1941 and 1946

—— Pies ——

Pie Crust
1 heaping cup shortening
3 cups flour   1 tsp. salt
3/4 cup cold water

Cut shortening into flour and salt until the mixture resembles coarse cornmeal. Add water, a little at a time, until the dough just holds together. Adding too much water will make the dough tough. Roll out dough on floured surface. Makes 2 double crust pies.
—Bertha Moody

No-Fail Pie Crust
5 cups flour   1 beaten egg
dash salt   1 tbsp. vinegar
1 lb. lard OR shortening

Combine egg and vinegar in measuring cup and add enough cold water to equal 1 cup liquid. In large bowl, cut shortening into flour. Add water, egg, vinegar and mix until dough is moist. This dough freezes well.
—Pat Caldwell

Meringue
2 egg whites   1 tsp. baking powder
3 tbsp. cold water   6 tbsp. granulated sugar
dash of salt

Combine egg whites, cold water and baking powder, and beat until stiff. Continue to beat and gradually add sugar and salt. Spread meringue on pie. Bake in preheated 425 degree oven. Remove after a few minutes, when meringue starts to brown.
—Thelma Kennedy

Fresh Strawberry Pie

1 quart fresh strawberries	2 tbsp. cornstarch
1 1/2 cups water	1 tbsp. oleo
3/4 cup sugar	1 tsp. vanilla
1 pkg. (3-oz.) strawberry jello	

Combine water, sugar and cornstarch in saucepan, and cook over medium heat until thickened. Remove from heat and add oleo, vanilla and jello. Mix and cool slightly. Slice strawberries and arrange in unbaked pie shell. Pour jello mixture over strawberries and chill until firm.
—Betty Dyer

Fresh Rhubarb Pie

2 cups chopped rhubarb	1 tsp. salt
2 eggs	1/3 tsp. nutmeg
1 tbsp. tapioca	1 cup sugar

Place chopped rhubarb in saucepan and cover with water. Bring water to steaming and immediately drain rhubarb. Beat eggs; add sugar, tapioca, salt and nutmeg. Add rhubarb and pour batter into unbaked, 9-inch pie shell. Cover with top crust and pinch crusts together. Bake 45 minutes at 350 degrees.
—Bertha Moody

Rhubarb-Orange Cream Pie

3 eggs, separated	1/4 cup flour
1 1/4 cups sugar	1/4 tsp. salt
1/4 cup softened oleo	2 1/2 cups chopped rhubarb
3 tbsp. orange juice	1/3 cup pecans

Combine oleo and orange juice with egg yolks and beat thoroughly. Add 1 cup sugar, flour and salt; beat well. Add rhubarb and stir. Add remaining sugar to egg whites and beat until stiff. Fold beaten egg whites into rhubarb batter and pour into unbaked, 9-inch pie shell. Sprinkle with nuts. Bake 15 minutes on bottom rack of 375 degree oven, then reduce heat and bake 40-45 minutes longer.
—Ona Moody

Dot Aho Moody

Butter Pie

2 eggs	1/4 tsp. salt
2/3 cup sugar	2 tbsp. melted oleo
2 tbsp. flour	1- 1 1/2 tsp. vanilla
1 1/2-2 cups milk	

Beat eggs in large bowl. In separate bowl, combine sugar, flour and salt, and add to eggs. Mix well. Add butter, salt and milk. Mix thoroughly. Pour batter into unbaked, 9-inch pie shell. Bake 15 minutes at 400 degrees, then reduce heat to 300 and cook 25-30 minutes longer. Makes one 9-inch pie.
—Bertha Moody

Pumpkin Pie

5 eggs, well beaten	1 tsp. nutmeg
1 1/2 cups sugar	1 tsp. salt
1 1/2 tsp. cinnamon	2 cups cooked pumpkin
1/2 tsp. cloves	1 can (12 oz.) evaporated milk

Mix together eggs, sugar, spices and salt. Beat well. Add pumpkin and milk. Stir well and pour batter into unbaked, 9-inch pie shell. Bake 15 minutes at 400 degrees, then reduce heat to 325 and cook 45-60 minutes longer. Pie is done when a knife inserted in the center comes out clean.
—Laura Jones

Pumpkin Pie II

1 cup sugar	1/2 tsp. salt
1 tbsp. cornstarch	1 3/4 cups cooked pumpkin
1/2 tsp. cinnamon	1 1/2 tbsp. melted oleo
1/2 tsp. ground ginger	1 1/2 cups milk
1/2 tsp. ground nutmeg	1/8 cup molasses
2 beaten eggs	

Sift together sugar, cornstarch, salt, cinnamon, ginger and nutmeg. Stir in pumpkin. Add eggs, oleo, molasses and milk. Pour batter into unbaked, 9-inch pie shell. Bake 15 minutes at 400 degrees, then reduce heat to 350 and bake 50 minutes.
—Jean Moody

Peanut Butter Pie

1 pkg. (8 oz.) softened cream cheese	1 cup powdered sugar
1/2 cup chunky peanut butter	1 container (12 oz.) cool whip
1 chocolate cookie crust	

Cream together peanut butter, cream cheese and sugar. Fold in cool whip and pour batter into chocolate crust. Refrigerate until serving, or freeze and serve frozen. Top with hot fudge and whipped cream.
--Judy Moody Beck

Nancy Moody Genthner

Old-Fashioned Cream Pie

3 cups flour   2 tsp. cream of tartar
1 1/3 cups shortening   1/2 tsp. salt
1 tsp, baking soda   1 tbsp. sugar
3/4 cup milk

Cut shortening into dry ingredients and add milk; mix well. Roll out dough and place on shallow, 10-inch ironstone plate. Trim edges. Bake dough about 10 minutes at 400 degrees, until lightly browned. Slide crust onto rack to cool. Makes four crusts.

Cream Filling: 1 cup sugar   1/2 tsp. salt
1/2 cup flour   2 cups milk
1 egg   1 tsp. vanilla

Combine sugar, flour and salt with beaten egg. Heat milk in top of double boiler. Once hot, add 1/4 cup to beaten egg mixture. Mix well and stir into remaining hot milk. Stir until thickened. Remove from heat and add vanilla. Cool filling. To assemble pie, place one crust on plate and cover with 1/2 the cream. Top with second crust.
—Bertha Moody

Lemon Sponge Pie

1/3 cup lemon juice and grated rind   3 heaping tbsp. flour
1 1/2 cups sugar   3 separated eggs
1 tbsp. melted oleo   1 1/2 cups milk

Beat together juice, sugar, oleo, flour and egg yolks. Add milk and stir. Beat egg whites until stiff and fold into batter. Pour into unbaked, 9-inch pie shell and bake 30 minutes at 350 degrees.
—Ona Moody

Apple Cranberry-Raisin Pie

5 large apples, about 2 3/4 lbs., thinly sliced
2 tbsp. oleo   1/2 cup diced raisins
1 cup cranberries   3 tbsp. flour
3/4 cup sugar   1 1/2 tsp. lemon peel OR
dash of lemon juice

Toss together all ingredients to coat well. Pour into unbaked, 9-inch pie shell and cover with top crust. Cut vents in top crust. Bake 10 minutes at 450 degrees then reduce heat to 350 and bake 30-40 minutes longer.
—Jan Jones

Little Pecan Pies

1/2 lb. butter	2 eggs
6 oz. softened cream cheese	1 1/2 cups brown sugar
2 cups flour	2 tbsp. melted butter
1 cup coarsely chopped pecans	dash salt
	1/2 tbsp. vanilla

Using pastry blender, mix together cream cheese, flour and butter until well blended. Press 1-inch balls of pastry into miniature cupcake tins, forming crusts. Combine and blend together remaining ingredients for filling. Fill cupcake tins half-full. Bake 15 minutes at 350 degrees, reduce heat to 250 and cook 10 minutes longer.
—Dorothy Bruns Moody

MOODY'S DINER
LUNCH   MENU

---HOT DRINKS---
Chocolate ...... Coffee ...... Tea
Malted Milk ...... Postum

---SANDWICHES---
ALL TOASTED SANDWICHES 5c EXTRA

Ham .. 10c	Ham & Eggs .. 20c
Bacon .. 10c	Bacon & Egg .. 20c
Cheese .. 10c	Fried Egg .. 10c
Hamburg, steamed rolls 10c	
Eastern .. 20c	Western .. 20c
Chicken 20c	Cream Cheese 10c
Cream Cheese & Nut 15c	
Cream Cheese & Olive 15c	
Cream Cheese & Date 15c	
Peanut Butter 10c	
Lobster .. 20c	Crabmeat .. 20c
Ham & Cheese 15c	
Salmon Salad 15c	
Bread & Butter 5c	
Chopped Ham, mayonnaise 10c	

We serve hot meat sandwiches
Any Combination Sandwich will be made on request.

Sandwiches to take out
(over)

**MOODY'S
HOME MADE ICES**
French Vanilla - Chocolate
Strawberry,
fresh berries in season
Caramel,   Coffee,   Banana
Butter Pecan,   Grape Nut
Orange Pineapple,   Cherry
Pineapple Pistachio
Frozen Pudding

---SUNDAES---
Marshmallow, Cherry ....
.... Chocolate 10c - 15c
Pineapple, Strawberry 10c-15c
Butterscotch .... 10c - 15c
Banana Splits.... 10c & 20c size
Walnuts & Pecans.. ....10c - 15c

---MILK DRINKS---
Plain Milk 5c Milk Shakes 10c
Malted Milk 10c   Velvets 15c
Egg & Milk 15c
Egg & Malted Milk 15c
All Kinds of Cold Sodas
Come in and see our Breakfast
and Dinner Menu.
(over)

Moody's Diner Menu from the 1930's
(front and back)

Cakes

Apple Cake

2 medium apples, peeled and chopped
1 cup sugar   1/2 tsp. nutmeg
1 1/2 cups flour   1/2 tsp. allspice
1 tsp. baking soda   1/2 cup melted oleo
1/2 tsp. salt   1 egg
1 tsp. cinnamon   1/2 cup raisins
1/2 cup chopped nuts

Place apples in large bowl; add sugar and let stand 10 minutes. Blend melted oleo and unbeaten egg into apples. Sift flour, spices, soda and salt and stir into batter. Fold in raisins and nuts. Pour into greased 8-inch pan and bake 40-50 minutes at 350 degrees. Cool cake in pan 10 minutes before removing.
—Marge Adams

Fresh Apple Cake

5 or 6 med. apples, peeled   1 tsp. nutmeg
2 cups sugar   1 tsp. baking soda
1 cup oil   1 tsp. salt
2 eggs   3 cups flour
2 tsp. cinnamon   1 cup chopped nuts

Slice apples into large bowl. Add sugar, oil and eggs and mix by hand. Let batter set while sifting dry ingredients. Mix dry ingredients into batter, then add nuts. Mix well and pour into 13 x 9 pan. Bake 40 minutes at 350 degrees. Serve warm with whipped cream.
—Judy Moody Beck

Melt-In-Your-Mouth Blueberry Cake

4 eggs, separated   1/2 tsp. salt
2 cups sugar   3 cups flour
1 cup shortening   2 tsp. baking powder
2 tsp. vanilla   2/3 cup milk
3 cups blueberries

Beat egg whites until stiff, then fold in 1/2 cup sugar and set aside. Dust blueberries with 1 tbsp. flour and set aside. Cream shortening, add salt, vanilla and remaining sugar. Add egg yolks and beat until creamy. Sift dry ingredients and add to batter alternately with milk. Fold in beaten egg whites and blueberries. Turn batter into well-greased 9 x 13 pan and sprinkle with sugar. Bake 55 minutes at 350 degrees.
—Margaret Moody Wellman

Carrot Cake

2 cups flour   1 tsp. baking powder
1 cup honey OR   2 tsp. nutmeg
2 cups sugar   1/2 tsp. salt
1 1/4 cup oil   4 eggs
2 tsp. cinnamon   3 cups grated carrots
1 cup combined nuts & raisins, optional

Combine dry ingredients, and add honey (or sugar) and oil. Add eggs one at a time, mixing well each time. Stir in carrots, nuts and raisins. Pour batter into a greased and floured 9 x 13 pan. Bake 30-40 minutes at 350 degrees, or until cake tester comes out clean. Cool and frost with cream cheese frosting.

Cream Cheese Frosting

Cream together one stick of softened oleo with 1 pkg. (8 oz.) of softened cream cheese. Beat in either honey to taste or 1 lb. powdered sugar. Use your imagination for flavorings: rum, almond or vanilla extracts, orange peel or nuts.
—Brian Moody

Carrot Cake II

1 cup oil   2 tsp. baking powder
2 cups sugar   2 tsp. baking soda
4 eggs   1 tsp. cinnamon
3 cups grated carrots   1 tsp. vanilla
2 cups flour   1 cup chopped nuts, optional

Mix together oil and sugar; add eggs and carrots, and mix well. Add dry ingredients and mix thoroughly. Add vanilla and nuts. Pour batter into a greased and floured 9 x 13 pan and bake 1 hour, 10 minutes at 300 degrees.

Frosting for Carrot Cake II

3 oz. softened cream cheese   1 tsp. instant coffee
1/2 stick softened oleo   1 tsp. vanilla
powdered sugar

Cream oleo and cream cheese; beat in coffee and vanilla. Add enough powdered sugar to make frosting thick enough to spread, and frost cake while still hot.
—Laura Jones

Patrick Downs

Easy Carrot Cake

1 cup sugar	1/2 tsp. salt
1 1/2 cups flour	1/2 cup chopped walnuts
3/4 cup oil	1/2 cup raisins
1 tsp. baking soda	2 eggs
1 tsp. cinnamon	1 jar baby food carrots

Mix together sugar, flour and oil. Stir in baking soda, cinnamon and salt. Add walnuts, raisins, eggs and carrots, and mix well. Pour batter into greased and floured 9-inch pan. Bake 35 minutes at 375 degrees, or until toothpick inserted comes out clean.

Easy Carrot Cake Frosting

1/4 cup softened oleo	1 tsp. vanilla
1 pkg. (3 oz.) softened cream cheese	2 1/4 cups powdered sugar

Combine all ingredients and beat until smooth.
—Jolene Millay

Zucchini Carrot Cake

2 eggs 1 tsp. baking soda
1 cup sugar 1 tsp. cinnamon
2/3 cup oil 1/2 tsp. salt
1 1/4 cups flour 1 cup grated carrots
1 tsp. baking powder 1 cup grated zucchini
1/2 cup chopped nuts

Beat together eggs and sugar, add oil and beat well. Add sifted dry ingredients and beat with electric mixer 3 minutes at high speed. Stir in carrots, zucchini and nuts. Pour into greased 9-inch pan and bake 35 minutes at 350. Frost with cream cheese frosting.
—Nellie Moody Jones

Auntie's One-Egg Cake

1/3 cup shortening
1 cup sugar 2/3 cup milk
2 tsp. baking powder 1 tsp. vanilla
1/2 tsp. salt 1 egg
1 1/4 cups plus 2 tbsp. flour

Combine dry ingredients, add shortening, milk and vanilla. Beat 2 minutes on medium speed. Add egg and beat 2 minutes more. Bake 35-40 minutes at 350 degrees in a greased and floured 8-inch pan. Top with nutmeg sauce.

New England Nutmeg Sauce

1 cup sugar 1 tbsp. oleo
2 tbsp. flour 1 tsp. nutmeg or cinnamon
2 cups boiling water dash of salt

Combine sugar, flour and salt and mix well. Gradually add boiling water, stirring constantly. Pour into double boiler, add oleo and cook 5 minutes or until thickened. Remove from heat and stir in nutmeg. Serve over one-egg cake.
—Brian Moody

Hot Milk Cake

2 eggs 1 tsp. baking powder
1 cup sugar 1/2 cup boiling milk
1 cup flour 3 tbsp. oleo
1 tsp. vanilla

Beat together eggs and sugar. Sift dry ingredients and add to eggs. Add oleo to boiling milk and mix into batter. Stir in vanilla. Bake 30 minutes at 350 degrees in a greased and floured 8-inch pan.
—Arletta Flagg

Elizabeth's Cake

1, 2-layer white or yellow cake mix   1 cup shredded coconut
1 cup cooked vanilla pudding   1/2 cup crushed nuts
1 can (20 oz.) drained, crushed pineapple   1/2 cup chopped red cherries
1 12-oz. container cool whip

Bake cake mix in 9 x 13 pan, according to package directions. Cool, then spread pudding over cake. Spread pineapple over pudding and top with cool whip. Sprinkle cool whip with coconut, nuts and cherries.
—Rebecca Little

Mocha Cake

4 tbsp. oleo   1 tsp. baking soda
1 cup sugar   1/2 cup cocoa
1 cup buttermilk OR sour milk   1/4 cup strong coffee
1 1/2 cups flour   1 tsp. vanilla

Cream together oleo and sugar. Stir baking soda into milk and add to creamed ingredients. Sift flour and cocoa and stir into batter then mix in coffee and vanilla. Pour batter into a greased and floured 9-inch pan. Bake 35-40 minutes at 350 degrees.
—Arletta Flagg

Kaye's Pound Cake

5 eggs   3 cups flour
3 cups sugar   1/2 tsp. salt
1/2 cup oleo   1/2. baking powder
1/2 cup shortening   1 cup milk
1 tsp. lemon flavoring

Combine eggs, sugar, oleo and shortening, and beat until light and fluffy. Add sifted dry ingredients to batter alternately with milk and lemon. Pour into greased and floured angel food cake pan and bake 1 hour at 350 degrees.
—Rebecca Little

Chocolate Cake

1 cup oleo   1/2 cup buttermilk
1 cup hot water   2 cups sugar
1/2 cup cocoa   2 cups flour
1 tsp. baking soda   2 eggs, lightly beaten
1 tsp. vanilla

Combine oleo, hot water and cocoa in saucepan and bring to a boil. Stir baking soda into buttermilk and set aside. Mix sugar and flour in large bowl, and pour in heated ingredients. Beat well. Add eggs, vanilla and buttermilk/baking soda, and mix until smooth. Pour batter into a greased and floured 10 x15 baking pan. Bake 20 minutes at 400 degrees. Cool and then cover with chocolate frosting on next page.

Chocolate Cake Frosting

6 tbsp. oleo   1 1/2 cups sugar
6 tbsp. milk   1 cup chocolate chips

Combine oleo, milk and sugar in a saucepan, and boil rapidly for 30 seconds. Add chocolate chips and stir until frosting is smooth. Pour hot frosting over cake.
—Jean Moody

Filigree Devil's Food Cake

1 1/2 cups sifted flour   1 tsp. salt
1 1/4 cups sugar   2/3 cup shortening
1/2 cup cocoa   1 cup milk
1 1/4 tsp. baking soda   1 tsp. vanilla
1/4 tsp. cream of tartar   2 eggs

Sift flour, sugar, cocoa, soda, cream of tartar and salt into mixer bowl. Drop in shortening. Add 2/3 cup milk and vanilla and beat 2 minutes on medium speed. Scrape bowl continuously while mixing. Add eggs and remaining milk and beat 2 minutes longer. Pour batter into two, deep, 8-inch greased and floured pans and bake 30-40 minutes at 350 degrees.
--Marion Whitmore

Crazy Chocolate Cake

3 cups flour   1 tsp. salt
2 cups sugar   3/4 cup oil
6 tbsp. cocoa   2 tbsp. vinegar
2 tsp. baking soda   2 tsp. vanilla
2 cups water

Combine all ingredients and beat well. Pour batter into greased and floured 9 x 13 pan, and bake 40 minutes at 350 degrees. Frost with Fluffy Cocoa Frosting.

Fluffy Cocoa Frosting

3/4 cup cocoa   1 tsp. instant coffee
4 cups powdered sugar   1 tsp. vanilla
1/2 cup oleo   1/2 cup evaporated milk

Mix cocoa, sugar and coffee. Reserve 1/3 and cream the remainder together with the oleo. Blend in vanilla and half the milk. Add remaining cocoa-coffee mixture, and blend well. Add remaining milk to batter and beat to desired consistency.
—Brian Moody

Lazy Daisy Oatmeal Cake

1 cup dry oatmeal	2 eggs
1/4 cup boiling water	1 1/2 cups flour
1/2 cup oleo	1 tsp. baking soda
1 cup packed brown sugar	3/4 tsp. cinnamon
1 cup sugar	1/4 tsp. nutmeg
1 tsp. vanilla	dash of salt

Combine oatmeal and boiling water in small bowl and set aside for 20 minutes. Beat together oleo, sugars, vanilla and eggs. Add dry ingredients, then add oatmeal. Pour batter into greased and floured 9 x 13 pan and bake 35-40 minutes at 350 degrees.

Frosting:

1/4 cup oleo	3 tbsp. water
1/2 cup brown sugar	1/3 cup chopped nuts
3/4 cup coconut	

Combine oleo, sugar and water in saucepan and heat until melted. Add nuts and coconut, mix well and pour over cooled cake.
—Susan Moody

Snackin' Cake

1 2/3 cups flour	1/3 cup vegetable oil
1 cup brown sugar	1 tsp. vinegar
1 tsp. baking soda	3/4 cup dry oatmeal
1/2 tsp. salt	1 tsp. allspice
1 cup water	2 tbsp. molasses
1/2 cup raisins	

Mix together dry ingredients. In large bowl, combine molasses, water, oil and vinegar. Mix in dry ingredients and raisins. Pour batter into 8-inch baking pan and bake 35-40 minutes at 350 degrees.
—Nancy Moody Genthner

Pistachio Nut Cake

1 box yellow cake mix	4 eggs
1/2 cup orange juice	1/2 cup oil
1/2 cup water	3/4 cup chocolate syrup
1 box instant pistachio nut pudding mix	

Combine mixes, orange juice, water, eggs and oil in mixing bowl. Beat with electric mixer 2 minutes on medium speed, until smooth. Pour 3/4 of the batter into a greased and floured tube pan. Add chocolate syrup to remaining batter and pour over batter in pan. Bake one hour at 350 degrees.
—Betty Dyer

Steve Heddericg

Celebrities at Moody's Diner

(left to right) Eda Hoak, Cynthia Hilton, Caroline Kennedy, Nadine Achorn, Avis Luce. (*The Weekly*, Waldoboro, Maine. February 14, 1980. Reprinted by permission.) Eda was a great fan of the Kennedy's. It was quite a thrill for her to meet Caroline. Eda came to the diner right after the war. She knew sign language and would take orders from people who were deaf. She knew everyone. Tourists and other travelers used to look for her whenever they came back.

Nellie: *Who was it that came in not long ago?*
Alvah: *I can't remember his name, he hosts a show and uses that long microphone. Gene Rayburn, that's him. He was sitting out there and Sheila kept wondering if he was who he looked like or not. So I said, "Go ask him." She went right up to him and said, "Are you the real thing or do you just look like him?" "No," he said, "I'm the real thing."*
Nellie: *His wife, or whoever was with him, said he didn't mind people asking for his autograph. That was nice of him.*
Alvah: *He had a great, big camper with a Lincoln hooked behind it. If she'd seen that she'd have known he wasn't a look-alike.*
Bill: *Then there was the guy from Gilligan's Island.*
Alvah: *Bob Denver I think his name is. Gary Merrill used to be in quite often.*
Bill: *Gorgeous George the Wrestler was in not long ago.*

Tomato Soup Cake

1 cup sugar	1 tsp. cinnamon
1/2 cup shortening OR lard	1 tsp. cloves
1 tsp. baking soda	1 tsp. nutmeg
1 can (12 oz.) tomato soup	1 tsp. salt
2 cups flour	1 cup seeded raisins
2 tsp. baking powder	1 cup walnuts

Beat together sugar, shortening and baking soda. Add tomato soup and mix well. Sift dry ingredients and add to batter. Mix well. Stir in raisins and nuts. Pour batter into greased and floured 9 x 13 pan. Bake 45 minutes at 350 degrees, or until toothpick inserted in center of cake comes out clean.
—Doris Moody Eaton

Squash Cupcakes

1 cup sugar	1 tsp. salt
2 eggs	1 tsp. ginger
1/2 cup shortening	1 tsp. nutmeg
2 cups flour	1 tsp. cinnamon
1 tsp. baking soda	1/4 - 1/2 cup buttermilk
1 tsp. baking powder	1 tsp. vanilla
1 1/2 cups squash	

Cream together sugar, eggs and shortening. Sift dry ingredients and add to creamed eggs-shortening. Add milk, vanilla and squash, and stir well. The amount of buttermilk used depends upon the moisture of the squash. It's better to use too much buttermilk than too little. Pour batter into lined muffin tins, 3/4-full, and bake 15-20 minutes at 350 degrees. Frost with favorite icing.
—Debbie Moody Bellows

—— Cookies ——

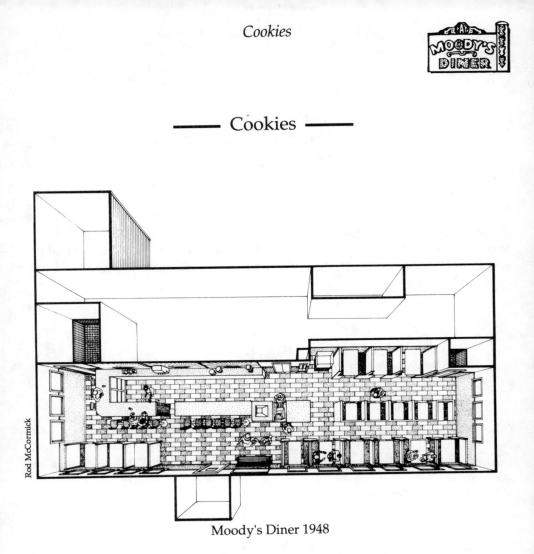

Rod McCormick

Moody's Diner 1948

Mom's Fat Molasses Cookies

1/2 cup sugar	1/2 tsp. salt
1/2 cup shortening	1/2 tsp. cinnamon
1/2 cup molasses	1/2 tsp. ginger
1/2 cup buttermilk OR sour milk	1 rounded tsp. baking soda
2 1/4 cups flour	

Cream together sugar and shortening. Add sour milk and molasses, and mix well. Stir in dry ingredients. Let dough set in refrigerator for 30 minutes. Roll out to 1/2-inch thick and cut with round biscuit cutter. Place on cookie sheet and sprinkle with sugar. Bake 15-20 minutes at 350 degrees.
—Nancy Moody Genthner

McGintey Cookies

3/4 cup shortening	1/2 tsp. baking powder
2 cups brown sugar	1 tsp. salt
2 eggs	1 tsp. baking soda
1/2 tsp. vanilla	3/4 cup chopped walnuts
2 cups flour	4 tbsp. milk

Cream shortening and sugar; add eggs and vanilla, and beat well. Sift together dry ingredients and add to batter, alternating with milk. Fold in nuts and drop by table-spoons onto greased cookie sheet. Bake 15 minutes at 325 degrees.
—Nellie Moody Jones

Date Balls

1 cup chopped dates	1 beaten egg
1 cup sugar	grated coconut OR
1/4 cup shortening	powered sugar
2 1/2 cups Rice Krispies	

Combine and boil sugar, dates, shortening and egg until sugar completely dissolves — about 2 minutes. Remove from heat and stir in Rice Krispies. Mix well. When mixture cools enough to handle, shape into walnut-sized balls. Roll in coconut or powdered sugar.
—Nancy Moody Genthner

Grammy Moody's Hermits

1 cup sugar	3 cups flour
1/2 cup oleo or shortening	1/2 tsp. cinnamon
2 eggs	1 tsp. salt
1/2 cup buttermilk	1/2 tsp. nutmeg
1 tsp. baking soda	1/2 tsp. cloves
1 cup chopped raisins	

Cream together sugar and shortening. Add eggs and buttermilk, and mix thor-oughly. Sift dry ingredients and stir into batter, then fold in chopped raisins. Drop by teaspoons onto greased cookie sheet. Bake 12-15 minutes at 350 degrees.
—Nellie Moody Jones

Peanut Butter Bars

1/2 cup shortening	1/4 cup milk
1/2 cup sugar	1 cup flour
1/2 cup brown sugar	1/2 tsp. baking soda
1/3 cup peanut butter	1/2 tsp. salt
1 tsp. vanilla	1 cup rolled oats
1 egg	

In large bowl, cream shortening, sugar, brown sugar, peanut butter and vanilla. Add beaten egg and milk, and mix well. Sift together dry ingredients and stir into batter. Pour into 8-inch pan and bake 20-25 minutes at 350 degrees. Cool and frost with Cocoa Frosting. Cut cake into squares and serve.

Cocoa Frosting

2 cups powdered sugar
2-3 tbsp. boiling water
1/4 cup cocoa
1/2 tsp. vanilla
3 tbsp. oleo

Combine all ingredients and beat until creamy.
—Nancy Moody Genthner

The author at age 2.

Quick and Easy Brownies

These brownies are best underbaked a little.

1/3 cup softened oleo	2 squares of
1 cup sugar	unsweetened chocolate
2 eggs	1 tsp. vanilla
1/2 cup flour	1/4 tsp. salt
1 cup chopped walnuts	

In large bowl, cream oleo and sugar. Add eggs, melted chocolate, flour, salt, vanilla and nuts. Beat well. Pour batter into a greased and floured 8-inch baking pan. Bake 30 minutes at 300 degrees.
---Nancy L. Moody

Aunt Bertha's "By Cracky" Bars

1 cup sugar	1 tsp. salt
3/4 cup shortening	1/4 tsp. baking soda
2 eggs	1/2 cup chopped nuts
1 tsp. vanilla	1 square unsweetened chocolate, melted
1/3 cup milk	1 pkg. (6 oz.) semisweet chocolate chips
1 3/4 cups flour	6-10 whole graham crackers

Cream together sugar, shortening, eggs and vanilla. Add milk and mix well. Sift dry ingredients and stir into eggs and milk. Pour 1/3 of the batter into a small bowl and add melted chocolate and nuts. Spread into 13 x 9 baking pan. Layer graham crackers on top. Mix chocolate chips into remaining batter and spread over crackers. Bake 25 minutes at 375 degrees. Cool, then cut into squares.
These bars get a little dry if overcooked.
—Eleanor Chase

Whoopie Pies

3/4 cup oleo	3 cups flour
1 1/2 cups sugar	3/4 cup cocoa
2 eggs	3/4 tsp. baking powder
1/2 tsp. vanilla	2 1/4 tsp. baking soda
1 1/2 cups milk	1/2 tsp. salt

In large bowl, cream oleo, sugar, eggs and vanilla. Add milk slowly and mix well. Combine dry ingredients and stir into batter. Drop batter by the teaspoon onto a greased cookie sheet and bake 15 minutes at 350 degrees. Cool, then fill with Whoopie Pie filling.

Whoopie Pie Filling:

1 cup milk	1/2 cup oleo
6 tbsp. flour	1 cup sugar
1/2 cup shortening	2 tsp. vanilla

Cook milk and flour in saucepan until thickened. Cool, and beat in remaining ingredients. Beat until filling is light and fluffy.
—Susan Moody

Molasses Whoopie Pies

1 cup sugar	1 tsp. vinegar
1 cup shortening	4 1/2 cups flour
1 tsp. salt	1 tsp. cinnamon
2 eggs	1 tsp. ground ginger
1 cup molasses	2 tsp. baking soda
1 cup hot, strong coffee	

Combine and cream sugar, shortening and salt. Add eggs, molasses and vinegar, and mix thoroughly. In separate bowl, sift together flour, cinnamon and ginger, and stir into batter. Dissolve baking soda in hot coffee and add to remaining ingredients. Drop by the teaspoonful onto a greased cookie sheet and bake 15 minutes at 350 degrees. Cool and fill with marshmallow filling.

Marshmallow Filling:

1/2 cup shortening	1 cup powdered sugar
4 tbsp. marshmallow fluff	milk

Combine all ingredients and beat thoroughly; add just enough milk to make frosting spreadable.
—Nellie Moody Jones

Mom's Old-fashioned Filled Cookies

1/2 cup shortening	1 tsp. vanilla
1 cup sugar	3 cups flour
1 egg	1 tsp. salt
1/2 cup milk	2 1/2 tsp. baking powder

Combine and cream sugar and shortening. Beat in egg, milk and vanilla. Sift dry ingredients; add to batter and mix well. Roll dough to 1/4-inch thick and cut cookies with round cutter. Put cookies on large cookie sheet and drop filling into the center of each. Top with second cookie and seal edges lightly. Bake 10 minutes at 350 degrees.

Mom's Old-fashioned Cookie Filling

1 box (8-oz.) chopped dates	1 tbsp. flour
1/2 cup water	1/2 tsp. salt
1/2 cup sugar	1/2 tsp. vanilla

Combine all ingredients and cook over medium heat until thickened.
—Nancy Moody Genthner

Gingersnaps

1/2 cup shortening	2 cups flour
1/4 cup soft oleo	1 tsp. ground ginger
1 cup sugar	2 tsp. baking soda
1 egg	1 tsp. cinnamon
1/4 cup molasses	1/2 tsp. salt

Cream shortening, oleo and sugar, then add egg and molasses. Mix well. Sift dry ingredients and stir into batter. Shape into small balls and roll in sugar. Place on cookie sheet and bake 10-12 minutes at 350 degrees, being careful not to overbake. Gingersnaps are done when soft and puffy.
—Corinne Perkins

100 Good Cookies

1 egg	1 tsp. vanilla
1 cup oil	3 1/2 cups flour
1 cup oleo	1 cup Rice Krispies
1 cup brown sugar	1 cup rolled oats
1 cup granulated sugar	1 cup chocolate chips
1 cup chopped walnuts	

Cream together first 5 ingredients. Add remaining ingredients and mix well. Drop batter by the spoonful onto ungreased baking sheets and bake 12-15 minutes at 350 degrees. Coconut, butterscotch bits, peanut butter bits or raisins can be substituted for the chocolate chips, walnuts or both.
—Charlene Ward

Chocolate Crinkles

4 squares unsweetened chocolate, melted

1/2 cup oil	2 tsp. vanilla
2 cups granulated sugar	2 cups sifted flour
4 eggs	1/2 tsp. salt
2 tsp. baking powder	

Mix oil and sugar together; stir in melted chocolate. Beat in eggs, one at a time. Add vanilla, and stir in flour, baking powder and salt. Chill batter several hours in refrigerator before using; overnight is best. Drop by the spoonful into powdered sugar and roll to coat. Place cookies 2 inches apart on greased cookie sheet. Bake 10-12 minutes at 350 degrees, being careful not to overbake.
—Corinne Perkins

Cocoa Drop Cookies

1/2 cup softened shortening
1 egg   1/2 cup cocoa
1 cup sugar   1/2 tsp. salt
1 tsp. vanilla   1/2 tsp. baking soda
3/4 cup milk   1 3/4 cups sifted flour

Beat together shortening, egg and sugar. Stir in milk and vanilla. Sift remaining ingredients, add to batter and mix thoroughly. Chill at least 1 hour. Drop batter by the spoonful onto greased baking sheet, about 2 inches apart, and bake 8-10 minutes at 400 degrees.
—Brenda Post

Thick Molasses Cookies

These are very soft cookies.

1 egg   1/2 tsp. salt
1/2 cup sugar   1/4 tsp. cloves
1/4 cup shortening   1 tsp. cinnamon
2/3 cup molasses   1/2 tsp. ginger
1/2 cup buttermilk OR   2 tsp. baking powder
sour milk   2 1/2 cups flour
1 tsp. baking soda dissolved in buttermilk

Cream egg, shortening and sugar; add molasses and mix well. Stir in buttermilk and soda, and add sifted dry ingredients. Mix well. Let batter rest about 30 minutes, then turn batter onto floured surface and roll thick. Cut with round cutter and bake 20 minutes at 350 degrees.
—Nellie Moody Jones

Cream-filled Oatmeal Cookies

1/2 cup shortening   1/4 tsp. ginger
3/4 cup brown sugar   1/4 tsp. cloves
2 eggs   scant tsp. salt
1/3 cup molasses   2 cups rolled oats
1 tsp. baking soda   1 3/4 cups wheat flour
1/2 tsp. cinnamon   1/4 cup milk

Cream together shortening and brown sugar. Then beat in eggs and molasses. Add baking soda, spices and salt, and mix well. Stir in oats, flour and milk. Drop batter by the spoonful onto greased cookie sheet. Flatten with fork and bake 10-12 minutes at 350 degrees. Use filling on next page.

Oatmeal Cookie Cream Filling:

1/3 cup shortening   1 cup powdered sugar
3 heaping tbsp. marshmallow fluff

Combine all ingredients and mix well, adding enough milk to make filling spreadable.
—Debbie Moody Bellows

Oatmeal Plus Cookies

1/2 cup sugar	1/2 cup oleo
1/2 cup brown sugar	1/2 cup shortening
1/4 cup peanut butter	1 1/2 cups flour
2 eggs	1 tsp. baking soda
1 tsp. vanilla	2 cups rolled oats
2 ripe bananas, mashed	1 cup chocolate chips

Cream together sugar, eggs, vanilla and bananas. Stir in remaining ingredients and mix well. Drop batter by the spoonful onto cookie sheet and bake 10-15 minutes at 375 degrees. Peanut butter chips, butterscotch bits or coconut can be substituted for chocolate chips.
—Debbie Moody Bellows

Cynthia's Peanut Butter Cookies

1/2 cup sugar	1 1/2 cups flour
1/2 cup brown sugar	1 tsp. baking soda
1 egg	1/4 tsp. salt
1/2 cup oleo	1/4 tsp. baking powder
1/2 cup peanut butter	

Cream together sugars and oleo, then beat in egg and peanut butter. Mix in dry ingredients. Drop batter by teaspoons onto cookie sheet and flatten with fork. Bake 8-10 minutes at 350 degrees.
—Nancy Moody Genthner

Double Peanut Butter Cookies

3 cups flour OR 2 cups flour & 1 cup quick oatmeal
1 cup sugar   1 cup oleo
1 tsp. baking soda   1 cup creamy peanut butter
1/2 tsp. salt   2 tbsp. milk
1/2 cup light corn syrup

Sift together dry ingredients. Using pastry blender, cut in oleo and peanut butter until dry ingredients resemble cornmeal. Blend in corn syrup and milk. Shape dough into 2 rolls and chill. (I shape mine so the cookies will be rectangular when cut.) Slice chilled dough 1/4-inch thick and place half the slices on ungreased cookie sheet. Spread dough slices with 1/2 tsp. crunchy peanut butter and cover with second slice. Bake 8-10 minutes at 350 degrees, being careful not to overbake. Cool slightly before removing cookies from pan.
—Judy Moody Beck

Salted Peanut Cookies

2 eggs   1 tsp. baking soda
2 cups packed brown sugar   1 tsp. baking powder
1 1/2 cups melted oleo   1/2 tsp. salt
1 1/2 cups salted Spanish peanuts   3 cups rolled oats
2 1/2 cups flour   1 cup cornflakes

Combine eggs and sugar, and beat well. Blend in melted oleo, then stir in peanuts. Set aside. Sift flour, soda, baking powder and salt into large bowl. Add rolled oats and cornflakes. Stir dry ingredients into batter and mix well. Drop by the spoonful onto greased cookie sheets and bake 8-10 minutes at 400 degrees. Remove cookies from pan at once.
—Jean Moody

Sugar Cookies

1 1/2 cups sugar   4 tsp. cream of tartar
3/4 cup shortening   4 cups flour
2 eggs   1 tsp. salt
1/2 cup milk   2 tsp. baking soda
1 tsp. vanilla OR lemon extract

Cream shortening and sugar; add eggs and milk. Sift dry ingredients, add to batter and mix well. Chill 1 hour. Roll dough to 1/8-inch thick on floured surface and cut. Place cookies on ungreased baking sheet and bake 6-8 minutes at 350 degrees.
—Bertha Moody

Pineapple Sponge Cookies

1/3 cup shortening	1 1/3 cups flour
2/3 cup sugar	1/2 tsp. baking soda
1 egg	1/4 tsp. salt
1 tsp. lemon extract	1/2 cup crushed pineapple

Cream shortening with sugar, and beat in egg. Sift flour with baking soda and salt, and add to creamed batter. Fold in pineapple, lemon flavoring and mix lightly. Drop by the teaspoonful onto a greased cookie sheet and bake 12 minutes at 400 degrees.
—Deborah Pooley

Chunky Brownies with Crust

These brownies are delicious and not too sweet.

1 1/4 cup flour	1 egg
1/2 cup cold oleo	1/2 tsp. baking powder
1/4 cup sugar	1 tsp. vanilla
1 can (14 oz.) sweetened-condensed milk	1 bar (8 oz.) milk chocolate candy, broken into chunks
1/4 cup unsweetened cocoa	3/4 cup chopped nuts

In medium bowl, combine 1 cup flour and sugar. Cut in oleo until mixture is crumbly. Press crumbs firmly on bottom of 13 x 9 pan and bake 15 minutes at 350 degrees. In larger bowl, beat together milk, cocoa, egg, remaining flour, vanilla and baking powder. Stir in chocolate chunks and nuts, and spread batter over prepared and baked crust. Bake 30 minutes or until center is set. Cool and sprinkle with powdered sugar. To store, keep brownies tightly covered at room temperature.
—Marge Adams

Coffee Squares

2 eggs	1 tsp. salt
2 2/3 cups light brown sugar	1 tsp. baking soda
1 cup oil	3 cups flour
1 cup warm coffee	1 cup chopped walnuts
1 pkg. (12 oz.) semisweet chocolate chips	

Beat eggs in a large bowl; add sugar and oil and mix well. Stir in coffee, flour, soda and salt. Mix thoroughly and pour into greased 13 x 9 pan. Top with chocolate chips and walnuts. Bake 35-40 minutes at 350 degrees.
—Cathy Sprague

Coconut Pineapple Squares

1 1/4 cups crushed pineapple, drained   1 pkg. (6 oz.) semisweet chocolate chips
2-3 tbsp. pineapple juice   1/2 tsp. baking soda
1 cup coconut   2 eggs
1/2 cup shortening   2 cups flour
3/4 cup sugar   1/4 tsp. salt
1/4 tsp. ginger

Mix together 1/2 cup pineapple and coconut to make topping and set aside. Cream shortening, sugar and eggs. Sift dry ingredients and add to creamed ingredients. Stir in remaining pineapple and pineapple juice and add chocolate chips. Spread batter in greased and floured 9 x 13 pan and spread with topping. Bake 30 minutes at 350 degrees. Cool and cut into squares.
—Hannah Flagg

Carol's Chocolate Squares

2 sticks oleo   4 tbsp. cocoa
1 cup water

Combine these ingredients and bring to a boil; remove from stove and add:

2 cups flour   2 beaten eggs
2 cups sugar   1 tsp. vanilla

Pour into greased 13 x 9 pan and bake 20 minutes at 400 degrees. Remove from oven and frost.

Frosting:

1 stick oleo   1 box powdered sugar
4 tbsp. cocoa   1 tsp. vanilla
4 tbsp. milk   1/2 cup nuts

Melt and bring to a boil oleo, cocoa and milk. Remove from heat and quickly mix in sugar, vanilla and nuts. Spread over hot cake, then cool and cut in squares.
—Judy Moody Beck

Peanut Butter Fingers

1/2 cup oleo 1/2 tsp. baking soda
1/2 cup brown sugar 1/4 tsp. salt
1/2 cup sugar 1 cup flour
1 egg 1/2 tsp. vanilla
1/3 cup peanut butter 1 cup quick-cooking rolled oats
1 pkg. (6 oz.) semisweet chocolate chips

Topping:

1/2 cup powdered sugar 1/4 cup peanut butter
2-4 tbsp. milk

Cream oleo and sugars, and blend in egg and peanut butter. Add flour and oats, and mix well. Spread dough in ungreased 9 x 13 pan and bake 20-25 minutes at 350 degrees. Do not overbake. Remove from oven and sprinkle with chocolate chips. Let stand 5 minutes to melt, and spread. Combine topping ingredients and spread over cake.
—Norma Dion

Raspberry Chews

3/4 cup oleo 1 1/2 cups sifted flour
3/4 cup sugar 1 cup chopped walnuts
2 eggs, separated 1 cup raspberry preserves
1/2 cup flaked coconut

In large bowl, combine oleo with 1/4 cup sugar and beat until fluffy. Beat in egg yolks, blend in flour and spread in a 13 x 9 baking pan. Bake 15 minutes at 350 degrees or until crust is golden brown. Remove from oven and set aside. In separate bowl, beat egg whites until foamy — and double in volume. Beat in remaining sugar until meringue stands in firm peaks and fold in walnuts. Set aside. Spread raspberry preserves over baked crust and sprinkle with coconut. Spread meringue over raspberry-coconut layer and bake 25 minutes at 350 degrees. Cool and cut into squares.
—Margaret Moody Wellman

—— Candy ——

Peanut Butter Balls

1 cup oleo	1 tsp. vanilla
1/2 cup peanut butter	1 box (1 lb.) powdered sugar
1/2 cup chopped nuts	1 pkg. (12 oz.) semisweet chocolate chips
2/3 cup grated paraffin	

Melt oleo in medium saucepan. Add remaining ingredients, except chocolate and paraffin. Shape candy into small balls and chill. Melt together chocolate and paraffin in double boiler over hot — not boiling — water. Using two forks, dip peanut butter balls in chocolate and set on wax paper to dry.
—Sheri Beck

Brown Sugar Peanut Butter Fudge

2 cups sugar	3/4 cup milk
2 1/2 cups brown sugar	1 small jar peanut butter
1 jar (7 1/2 oz.) marshmallow fluff	

Boil together milk and sugars for 5 minutes. Remove from heat and add peanut butter and marshmallow. Spread in 9 x 13 pan and refrigerate until cool.
—Harriet Hilton

Peanut Butter Fudge

1 1/2 cups sugar	1/2 cup marshmallow fluff
6 tbsp. oleo	1/2 cup peanut butter
1/3 cup milk	1/4 cup chopped nuts, optional

Boil together milk, oleo and sugar for 4 minutes. Add peanut butter, marshmallow and chopped nuts. Stir to mix and spread in 8-inch square pan. Chill until firm.
—Sheri Beck

Three-Minute Fudge

1 cup sugar	1/2 cup milk
2 tbsp. cornstarch	3 tbsp. oleo
1 tbsp. cocoa	1 tsp. vanilla

Combine sugar, cornstarch, cocoa, milk and oleo and boil 3 minutes. Remove from heat; add vanilla and beat well. Pour into greased, 8-inch pan and chill until firm.
—Brenda Post

Reese's Squares

1 jar (18 oz.) peanut butter 1 cup sugar
1 jar (9 oz.) honey 5 tbsp. oleo
non-fat dried milk 1/3 cup millk
1 pkg. (6 oz.) semisweet chocolate chips

Blend together peanut butter and honey. Mix in dried milk until stiff. Press into 9 x 13 pan. In saucepan, combine sugar, oleo and milk. Bring to a boil, stirring constantly, for 1 minute. Remove from heat, stir in chocolate chips and blend until smooth. Spread over peanut butter and honey, and refrigerate until firm. Cut in squares to serve.
—Judy Moody Beck

Crunch Candy

1 cup butter 1/4 tsp. salt
1 cup sugar 1 lg. milk chocolate bar
2 tbsp. water 1 cup chopped nuts

Combine butter, sugar, water and salt in saucepan and heat, stirring constantly, to 300 degrees on candy thermometer — or until mixture forms brittle ball when dropped in cold water. Remove from heat and pour onto large, greased cookie sheet that has been warmed in the oven. Sprinkle chopped nuts and chocolate pieces on top. Cool and break into pieces.
—Rebecca Little

Mom's Party Mix

1/2 cup oleo 2 cups wheat Chex
4 tsp. Worcestershire sauce 2 cups Cheerios
1 tsp. seasoned salt 2 cups Kix cereal
2 cups rice Chex 2 cups thin pretzels
2 cups corn Chex 2 cups chinese noodles
1 cup salted peanuts

Over low heat, melt together oleo, Worcestershire sauce and seasoned salt. Mix cereals in large bowl and pour melted oleo over them. Stir well and pour mix onto greased cookie sheet. Bake 1 hour at 250 degrees, stirring every 15 minutes.
—Judy Moody Beck

Index